PROCLAMATION COMMENTARIES

• The Old Testament Witnesses for Preaching

Foster R. McCurley, *Editor*

EZEKIEL, SECOND ISAIAH

James Luther Mays

FORTRESS PRESS   Philadelphia, Pennsylvania

COPYRIGHT © 1978 BY FORTRESS PRESS

Library of Congress Cataloging in Publication Data

Mays, James Luther.
  Ezekiel, Second Isaiah.
  (Proclamation commentaries)
  Bibliography: p.
  Includes index.
    1. Bible. O.T. Ezekiel—Criticism, interpretation, etc. 2. Bible O.T. Isaiah XL-LV—Criticism, interpretation, etc. I. Title.
BS1545.2.M39   224'.1'06   77-15239
ISBN 0-8006-0592-6

6513J77   Printed in the United States of America 1-592

CONTENTS

3

EDITOR'S FOREWORD

This volume continues *Proclamation Commentaries–The Old Testament Witnesses for Preaching*. Like its New Testament counterpart, this series is not intended to replace traditional commentaries which analyze books of the Bible pericope by pericope or verse by verse. This six-volume series attempts to provide background material on selected Old Testament books which, among other things, will assist the reader in using *Proclamation: Aids for Interpreting the Lessons of the Church Year*. Material offered in these volumes consists of theological themes from various witnesses or theologians out of Israel's believing community. It is our expectation that this approach —examining characteristic themes and motifs—will enable the modern interpreter to comprehend more clearly and fully a particular pericope which contains or alludes to such a subject. In order to give appropriate emphasis to such issues in the brief form of these volumes, the authors present the results, rather than the detailed arguments, of contemporary scholarship.

On the basis of its concern to address the specific tasks of preaching and teaching the word of God to audiences today, this commentary series stresses the theological dilemmas which Old Testament Israel faced and to which her witnesses responded. Accordingly, the historical and political details of Israel's life and that of her ancient Near Eastern neighbors are left to other books. Selected for discussion here are those incidents and issues in Israel's history which have a direct relationship to the theological problems and responses in her existence. Since the word of God is always addressed to specific and concrete situations in the life of people, the motifs and themes in these commentaries are directed to those selected situations which best exemplify a certain witness's theology.

The concrete situation addressed by the theologians treated in this volume is the Babylonian Exile of the sixth century B.C. From 597 to 538 B.C. people of Judah, particularly of Jerusalem, experienced the trauma of separation from land and home. Because of their attempt to break loose from the yoke of Babylon, they were forced to live in the land of their masters in southern Mesopotamia. That was bad enough! But to make matters worse, some of those left behind at the first deportation in 597 revolted ten years later against the Babylonian King Nebuchadnezzar. This time the powerful ruler not only carted home more exiles but destroyed the Jerusalem temple and ravaged the city's walls.

The exile was obviously a historical matter which can be dated rather precisely and placed in a specific geographical area. The exile is also a sociological matter which can be discussed in terms of living arrangements, uncertainty about the future, strangeness in a new land, and longing for the good old days.

But most of all, the exile must be understood as a theological matter. The land promised by the Lord to Abraham had been wrenched away by a foreigner; the temple in which the Lord was believed to be present was nothing more than rubble; the Ark of the Covenant existed no more. Professor James Luther Mays illustrates in this book the type of questions the people raised about their relationship to God, his ability to keep his promises, the reasons for such tragedy, even the whereabouts and existence of God. Such theological problems and questions demand answers—also theological. To address those questions, or more precisely the people who raised such questions, God raised up his spokespersons, as he does in every age. These preachers to the exiles whose witness has been preserved for us were Ezekiel, the school of historians known as the Deuteronomists, the anonymous prophet we call Second Isaiah, and that circle of priests who gave us the final and framing strand of the Pentateuch.

It is the purpose of this volume to examine the two prophets of the exile whose preaching has had profound significance for the life of Israel and in the church: Ezekiel and Second Isaiah. Professor Mays approaches the Book of Ezekiel and Isaiah 40—55 in terms of the concrete situations each preacher faced and with special regard to messages directly related to those problems.

What is striking about Mays' treatment of these prophets is the emphasis he sees on "newness." In Ezekiel there is new life, new exodus, new saving history, new temple, new people. Likewise Second Isaiah promises a new exodus, a new Zion, a new messiah. And yet, as the author so clearly demonstrates, this newness is really a matter of reinterpreting the old traditions in such a way that they speak anew to the changed situation in the life of Israel. It is because of the past event when the Lord brought the slaves out of Egypt, through the wilderness, and to the Promised Land that the exilic prophets can point forward to a new exodus when the exiles will be taken home. It is due to the old traditions about Jerusalem and the temple that these spokespersons for God can describe in positive terms a new city and a new temple or a new Zion.

But because of their particular backgrounds and audiences, each of these prophets has his own emphases to make in the reinterpretation of old material. Such divergence is illustrated most dramatically by Mays in the treatment of the Davidic king. Among the serious issues raised by the exile and the destruction of Jerusalem was the Davidic covenant by which God promised that the lineage of David would occupy the throne of Jerusalem forever. The Davidic King Jehoiachin was carried away to Babylon in the first deportation in 597 B.C. and was kept prisoner there, apparently until his death. Thus ended the Davidic line which set one "messiah" after another on the throne for approximately three hundred years. Ezekiel, preaching early in the exilic period, addressed the question of leadership in the future by preaching that the Lord would reign and do the "shepherd's work" until he set up a new Davidic king in the future. Second Isaiah takes a completely different approach by designating the Persian King Cyrus as God's "messiah" and thus transferring the role of "anointed" ruler from the Davidides to a foreigner; actually David will play no role at all, for even the promises made to the Davidic line are transferred to the people of Israel.

Such is the dynamic quality of God's word to his people. His word takes different forms and expressions in order to meet new conditions. It is above all the word, asserts Professor Mays, that is primary in the work of these prophets. Visions, symbolic acts, and all else give way to the speaking and hearing of the word of God through prophecy.

At the same time Professor Mays treats here in characteristic clarity an issue which has been the subject of scholarly debate throughout this century: the identity of the servant in the four so-called Servant Songs of Second Isaiah. The oldest interpretation, indeed as old as the Septuagint itself, centers on a collective understanding by which the servant is Israel. Many scholars have regarded that identity to be problematic on several grounds, particularly because of the mission of Israel to Israel in Isaiah 49:1–6. And so the collective identity has given way in many circles to an individual interpretation. These approaches have taken two lines of development: a royal figure and a prophetic figure.

Nominations over the past century for a royal or kingly servant have included Uzziah, Hezekiah, Jehoiachin, and Zerubbabel. Apart from these historical figures, the king has sometimes been interpreted in mythological terms and linked to the ritual involving the king in the Babylonian New Year festival. And, of course, the royal image has contributed to the interpretation of the servant as the future Messiah.

Prophetic figures receiving the honors have been Moses, Isaiah, Jeremiah, Ezekiel, and Second Isaiah himself. Gerhard von Rad (*Old Testament Theology*, 2, pp. 250–262) argues that the evidence points to a future "prophet like Moses" who is not identifiable with persons in the preexilic and exilic periods.

Finally, the trend has come full circle with a new interpretation by which the servant is the cultic-center city of Zion-Jerusalem (see Leland W. Wilshire, *Journal of Biblical Literature* 94 [1975], pp. 356–367). The tasks of the four servant songs are argued to be fulfilled in the destruction and restoration of Zion-Jerusalem.

James Luther Mays is Professor of Biblical Interpretation at Union Theological Seminary, Richmond, Virginia. He is well known for his skill as a teacher and as an author, particularly for his volumes *Hosea, Amos* and *Micah* in The Old Testament Library published by Westminster Press. In addition, Dr. Mays serves as the editor of *Interpretation*, a journal devoted to the relevance of theological issues for the life of the church.

Fall, 1977   FOSTER R. MCCURLEY
                              Lutheran Theological Seminary at Philadelphia

This book is an introduction to the two prophets whose careers were set in the exilic period of Israel's history, Ezekiel and his unnamed colleague of Isaiah 40—55. It deals with the character of their prophetic work, the message they proclaimed, and the theology expressed in it. The book is designed to give its readers an orientation to these matters which will serve both as an invitation to and a context for their own interpretative work with these prophets. In planning what to include and what to omit, I have tried to be guided by the purpose of the book.

In much of the book I have concentrated on what the prophets said and have arranged the chapters around a discussion of specific passages selected because of their importance and typical character. The reality of prophecy is to be found in specific sayings; something of the reality is lost in generalizations and syntheses. This strategy allowed me also to deal with the texts from these two prophets which are used as Old Testament readings in the lectionaries. The book is thus a minor sort of commentary.

As a result of this strategy, discussion of critical questions of a historical and literary nature has been held to a minimum. I have given a concise summary of the problems raised by critical study, concentrating on those which affect interpretation the most. The works in the bibliography and the standard introductions to the Old Testament will furnish assistance in this area.

The book should be read with a Bible at hand and open. I have not, for the sake of saving space for comment, usually reproduced the text. If the reader will examine the passage under discussion before reading the section which deals with it and will refer to the text regularly in reading, it will greatly enhance the experience of study. Where I have quoted texts, they come from the Revised Standard Version.

The bibliography lists only those books which I would recommend for use to those who study Ezekiel and Isaiah 40—55 in preparation for preaching and teaching.

CHAPTER ONE

THE EXILIC PERIOD

The Babylonian Exile and the events which led to it brought a decisive change in Israel's political and religious history. The change was no less than a shift in eras. The old was passing away; something new was beginning. Israel started its historical career in Palestine as a tribal league, a social organization which served as a form for both its political and religious life. David transformed the tribal league into a national state organized as a monarchy. Jerusalem, with the temple built by Solomon, became the center of Israel's religious life, the goal of pilgrimages and the primary place for the worship of God. The Davidic kingship assumed a crucial role as the agency through which God provided protection, prosperity, and justice for his people. Israel's faith in the god who had called them to be his people and revealed his name Yahweh to them that they might call on him, became more and more a belief in city and temple and king.

In the early years of the sixth century B.C. Babylonian power brought the era of the monarchy in Judah to an end. When Nebuchadnezzar's troops had finished their work, Jerusalem had been razed to the ground, the temple plundered and left smoking rubble, and the reigning Davidic king captured and exiled to Babylon along with the religious and civil leadership of the nation. Judah's existence as an independent national state was over. It appeared that Judah and its people might suffer the fate brought on the state of Israel by the Assyrians and vanish from history. The future existence of Israel was put in jeopardy.

The crisis was total. It was theological as well as political. How and in what form Israel would exist as a community of faith was at issue. What Judah suffered was more than any corrective chastisement or painful purging. The entire structure of their corporate life was shattered. The disaster posed urgent questions for Israel's faith. Why had Israel's career as the people of Yahweh come to such a dismal end? What sense could be made of God's purpose now? How could they be kept alive as a community among the great states who had no place for their destiny? Was Yahweh really god in a way that transcended and negated the gods of the nations? Had he any power in this situation? Had they one and all really deserved such final catastrophe? Was Yahweh just? How was the righteousness of Yahweh to be vindicated against the ascendancy of the heathen? What now of the promise of the land, of the hope given through the anointed (messianic) king, of the assurance of God's presence among them in the temple, indeed of their election to be God's representative people in history? In the light of the miscarriage of their experience at being the people of God, was any such vocation possible for mortals? Who was equal to it?

Such questions hung over the ravaged countryside of Judah and formed in the minds of survivors who were left there and in the souls of the exiles who were carried away. The destruction of Jerusalem and the dispersal of its population seemed to have spelled the end to the Lord's way with Israel. Surely, it was the worst of times.

Yet, in a fashion so surprising as to invite the term miraculous, the exilic period turned out to be the best of times. It was a period of enormous importance in the formation of the biblical faith, comparable in significance to the time of the exodus from Egypt. Confronted with this imposing agenda of radical questions, certain individuals and groups within Israel found in their challenge the invitation to a renewed dialogue with Yahweh. The old traditions of Israel's faith were reassessed. Unsuspected dimensions of meaning were discovered which cast light on their dilemma, and became in turn the guide to recasting the traditions anew. Fresh impulses of inspiration came into the community through prophets, priests, and the wise. The faith of Israel was reformed and deepened in a way that laid foundations for the future. The possibility of Judaism as a religion independent of a national culture and of Christianity as an outcome of Old Testament faith was created in the exilic period.

Much of the literature of the Old Testament was produced or given its final form during the exile. The account of Israel's beginnings was revised, expanded, and put in its present form (Genesis–

Numbers). The history of Israel in the promised land was completed (Deuteronomy–II Kings). The sayings of the prophets who had proclaimed the warnings and promises which made theological sense of the final catastrophe were preserved, edited, and given permanent shape (Amos, Isaiah, Micah, Hosea, Jeremiah, and others). It is possible that the Book of Job reflects the spiritual wrestling of the time. In a real sense one could say that humanly speaking, the Old Testament itself is the achievement of Israel's response to the threat of its liquidation as a spiritual community.

There were two prophets whose careers belonged wholly to the exilic period. Indeed, both men were exiles in Babylon. The first is Ezekiel, who was active during the first quarter of the sixth century. The second is the unnamed prophet whose sayings are collected in chapters 40—55 of the Book of Isaiah. His ministry fell in the last decade or so of the exile. Together their prophecy spans the exilic period. Through them came the word of the Lord to interpret and illumine Israel's darkest hour. Their presence and proclamation showed the exiles that the faithfulness of Yahweh to his purpose was at work in their travail. The exile, in the broadest sense of the term, was both setting and subject of their prophecy. This book deals with their message and theology. From them we can learn how God is present in what can justifiably be called the death and resurrection of his people.

Like the prophets who preceded them, they spoke to Israel in the midst of the history through which they were living. Their words were not general or abstract, but messages from the Lord addressed to people in concrete circumstances. One essential for understanding their prophecy is a grasp of the history of the time and the way their ministries fit into its course.

The end of the seventh century (2 Kings 23:28—24:1). The events of the last decade of the seventh century prepared for what was to follow. Judah had enjoyed a respite from foreign domination during the period of Assyrian decline. When the state that had dominated the Near East for so long was overwhelmed by an alliance of Medes and Babylonians, a struggle ensued between Babylon and Egypt to gain control of Syria-Palestine. Josiah, the king who had sponsored the reformation of Judah's religious life under the influence of Deuteronomy, made the mistake of intervening. He opposed the Egyptians who were marching through Palestine in 609 and lost his life. His son, Jehoahaz, was displaced by Pharaoh Neco II to put Jehoiakim on the throne as his vassal. In 605 the Egyptians were defeated by the Babylonians at Carchemish and Hamath, and driven back to their borders. Jehoiakim immediately changed his allegiance and became a vassal of Nebuchadnezzar. The arrangement lasted only until Jehoiakim's first opportunity to break it. When the Babylonians failed in an attempt to invade Egypt in 601, Jehoiakim withdrew his allegiance. During all this time Jeremiah was active, announcing the judgment of God, calling Babylon the instrument of judgment, and opposing any dependence in Egypt.

The first deportation (2 Kings 24:1–20). The Babylonian army returned to Palestine in December of 598. Jehoiakim died in the same month. His son and successor, Jehoiachin, surrendered to Nebuchadnezzar in March 597. The royal family, the professional classes and leading citizens were taken to Babylon and settled in villages as a captive population. The king's uncle, Zedekiah, was made acting king. Jeremiah, who had opposed the rebellion, was allowed to remain in Jerusalem. He called on its population to accept the defeat as the work of God and said that the future of Israel lay with the exiles. He was not heeded. The Babylonians did not follow the Assyrian policy of scattering captive populations in other lands and settling alien people in their territory. The exiles were allowed to live as a community in their own villages in Babylon in a fashion that may have seemed a kind of temporary internment. Jehoiachin still lived, though a prisoner at the Babylonian court. If the situation were regarded as the judgment of Yahweh, it was understood as a chastisement now complete. Resistance and intrigue continued in Judah. There were prophets around who opposed Jeremiah and fanned the embers of hope. Ezekiel, who had been among the group deported, began his prophetic ministry among the exiles in 593. His stance was similar to Jeremiah's; he announced a terrible and final punishment yet to come on Jerusalem.

The second deportation (2 Kings 24:20—25:26). In 589 Judah joined Tyre and Ammon in rebellion, probably hoping for Egyptian help. Once again the Babylonian army returned. One by one the fortified cities of Judah were assaulted and taken. After a long seige Jerusalem fell in July 587. Zedekiah and another group of citizens were exiled. Nebuchadnezzar had the city razed, its walls pulled down, and the temple destroyed. The population had been decimated by fighting, hunger, flight, and deportation. A scattering of peasants was left to carry on life in the villages. All the institutions of Judah's national life were swept away. Judah as a state ceased to exist. Its territory became a province in the Babylonian Empire, Gedaliah was appointed governor, though there was not much to govern. But the stubborn resistance was not at an end. A group of zealots assassinated Gedaliah. In fear of reprisal, Gedaliah's associates fled to Egypt, taking Jeremiah with them. The fall of Jerusalem was the watershed of Ezekiel's prophecy. After the event, he took up the task of rebuilding a religious community among the exiles through messages of counsel and hope.

The exilic period (2 Kings 25:27–30; Ezra 1:1–4). The exile lasted until 538. What happened among the Israelites in Judah and Babylon during those years is unknown. The biblical account in 2 Kings breaks off after 587, and the books of Ezra and Nehemiah do not take up the story until the end of the period. The best way to learn the mood and circumstances of those who remained in Judah is to read the sobbing poetry of the Book of Lamentations. It re-creates in ways statistics cannot portray the devastation of city and spirit, the feeling of abandonment and grief which pervaded the land. In Babylon the exiles had to live with the loss of hopes that had been consumed in the fires that burned Jerusalem. Psalm 137 tells us that they found themselves unable to do more than lament when they gathered. Zion was a memory too painful to bear. Their resignation, despair, and bitterness are reflected in Ezekiel's sayings, who continued his work among them until as late as 571. Their prospects as a people and community of faith were discouraging. The invincible power of the Babylonian state and the imposing influence of its culture shut them up in a historical cul-de-sac. But in the space of little more than a decade a predicament that seemed permanent was resolved by an upheaval that changed their situation drastically. In 550 the Persian King Cyrus seized the Median Empire and launched a series of swift campaigns which brought one kingdom after another in the Near East under his dominion. While his triumphant progress was under way, the unnamed prophet of Isaiah 40—55 hailed Cyrus as the anointed of the Lord and began to proclaim a new salvation history for Israel. He summoned the exiles to prepare for a new exodus and return to their land. In 539 the Babylonian state collapsed with little resistance. A year later, Cyrus issued a royal decree which permitted the exiles to return to Judah. The exile was suddenly drawing to a close.

The work of Ezekiel and his prophetic colleague is to be understood against this background. Two more different prophets can hardly be imagined. Ezekiel was born to the priesthood; the traditions and perspectives of the sacral office inform his thinking and influence his style. The unknown prophet thought and spoke as one who was steeped in the language and craft of the hymns and prayers found in the Psalter. The first was severe, precise, and prosaic. The second was exhuberant, extravagant, and poetic to the highest degree. Their different styles seem appropriate to their task. The anticipation and aftermath of the death of Judah formed Ezekiel's setting. His younger colleague spoke when redemption was dawning on the horizon.

Along with these differences their prophecy shared a common basic structure. Though Ezekiel majored in the proclamation of judgment and his colleague in salvation, both sought to bring their community to accept its suffering as judgment. Both announced a new exodus toward Zion and its temple, were concerned with the obedience and redemption of those who would return, trusted in the power of the word of the Lord to bring this all to pass, and reshaped the messianic hope of their people. They sustained the spirit of the exiles with a summons to the life God would give them, and called them to a new form of existence as the people of God. They themselves were divine provision for a way through the darkness.

CHAPTER TWO

EZEKIEL AND HIS BOOK

The Lord called the son of Buzi to proclaim to the exiles in Babylon "words of lamentation and mourning and woe" (Ezek. 2:10). He was to persist in his unwelcome task, whether they heard or refused to hear, so that "they will know that there has been a prophet among them" (2:5). Ezekiel was a sign that the Lord was not through with what he had begun with the surrender of Jerusalem to Babylon, neither was he through with the exiles. To know that and to understand what it meant, the people needed a prophet.

In the period following the deportation of Jehoiachin and the upper classes of Judah, uncertainty prevailed. What would happen next? What was to be done? What did the situation mean for Israel's relationship to her God? Intrigue was rife in Jerusalem. The exiles were infected with the fever. Jerusalem and its temple still stood and the Davidic royal house had survived. Perhaps it was all temporary. Perhaps some way could be found to resume their old life. The one thing they could not accept was the radical implication of the message of judgment—that the Lord was saying a final "No" to what they had been. It was this blindness to what the Lord was doing and deafness to the word he was sending by Jeremiah that created the situation in which Ezekiel became a prophet.

THE MAN AND HIS BACKGROUND.

The Book of Ezekiel provides a sparse but clear outline of the prophet's career. He had been reared in one of the priestly families of Jerusalem (1:3). He must have been deported with the group of leading citizens who went into exile with King Jehoiachin in 597. The shock of that displacement drew a line through his life, and he dated reports of revelation that come to him in reference to that year (e.g. 1:2; 8:1). For five years he lived with his fellow Judeans who had been settled by the Babylonians in an abandoned village whose Babylonian name, *Til abūbī,* they pronounced Tel-abib. It was located on an arm of the Euphrates in the region of old Nippur (3:15). In 593, the glory of the Lord appeared to him, and through the vision he was commissioned to let a "Thus says Yahweh" be heard among the exiles.

From that point until Jerusalem was captured and razed in 587 he received revelations from the Lord and reported them to the exiles. Three times he notes that the elders of Israel were sitting before him in his house (8:1; 14:1; 20:1). The fact that they had come to seek a word of the Lord through him indicates he had the status of a prophet in the community. Probably most of his messages were delivered to those who came to his house. It is evident (see the discussion of the book below) that a coterie of disciples gathered about him. During this period he confronted all who would listen with the announcement that the end was coming for Judah. The loss of Jerusalem and its temple was the one fact the house of Israel must accept in order to grasp what their God was doing and to realize what the meaning of their relation to him was. Ezekiel spoke of the nearing calamity and enacted it in dramatic portrayals with a tempo that increased when Nebuchadnezzar responded to Zedekiah's rebellion, marched on the city, and put it under siege. During the long cruel months of the siege Ezekiel's wife died, and as a sign to the exiles that they must accept the loss of Jerusalem as the work of their God, he was instructed by God not to mourn her death (24:15ff.) On the threshold of the disaster he was struck dumb as if his prophetic task were finished. When the city fell, he was silent.

On the nineteenth of January in 586, six months after the walls were breached, a fugitive brought him word that his prophecy had been fulfilled, and his speech returned to him (33:21f.). The recovery of his capacity to speak marked a new phase of his career. When every human reason to hope had been shattered and all continuities with the past were broken, Ezekiel began to announce the re-creation of God's people. He lifted before the eyes of the exiles a vision of a future existence which God would bring about for his own glory, and bid them live in anticipation of that future. He received a second call, a redefinition of his office, in which the Lord made him a watchman responsible for the life and death of each individual committed to his care (33:1–9; the similar 3:16–21 is a version of the "second call" attached to the report of Ezekiel's first call in the redaction of the book).

The latest date given in the book is the twenty-seventh year of the exile (571). Ezekiel died in the community of exiles to whom he had prophesied for some quarter of a century, long before there was any tangible evidence that the new day he foresaw would dawn.

Ezekiel's nurture in the priestly tradition had a significant influence on his thought. Clearly he viewed and evaluated Israel's past and present from the perspectives characteristic of the priestly world of ideas. For him the temple in Jerusalem was the constitutive center of Israel's religious life, the place where the glory of the Lord dwelt (chaps. 8—11, 40—48). In describing the sin of Israel he talked primarily about failure in the sphere of the holy, about the abominations of uncleanness and idolatry. The norms he applied to Israel were often regulations which governed sacral matters (e.g. 16:1–12; 18). In these and other aspects of his thought he belongs to the same traditions which are found in the laws in Leviticus 17—26 and in the Priestly narrative of Israel's beginnings. He was well informed about the history of his own people (see the long surveys in chapters 16, 20, 23) and acquainted with a broad range of mythic themes at home in the intellectual world of the ancient Near East (e.g. the motifs in 28:11ff.; 31; 47). Such a range of knowledge might also have been acquired in the environment of a priestly family.

Though Ezekiel was born and trained for the priesthood, it was in the prophetic vocation that his heritage was reshaped and used. To a surprising extent, Ezekiel's predecessors in the prophetic succession live on in him. For all his distinctiveness, he revives and draws on the prophets of the past. It is particularly striking that many features of early prophecy reappear in his. He is much closer to Elijah and Elisha and their forerunners than any other writing prophet. The spirit of the Lord, hardly mentioned in classical prophecy, plays a major role in his experience, seizing and transporting him from one place to another (3:14f.; 8:3; 11:24). Like the old prophets, he feels "The hand of the Lord" upon him (1:3; 8:1; etc.). He is possessed, moved to a different realm of experience. He sees what is happening in distant places (chaps. 9—11, 40—48). His prophecy is accompanied by gestures and bodily movements which direct his message (e.g. 6:1; 13:17). Much that seems strange in Ezekiel is due to his inheritance of old prophetic practices.

But he is no less related to the prophets from Amos to Jeremiah. In fact he draws specifically on their words. A particular feature of Ezekiel's prophecy is the way he takes an image or sentence or theme from his predecessors and, by expanding and elaborating it, creates an extended saying of his own (compare Amos 8:1ff. with Ezek. 7; Hos. 2 with Ezek. 16; Isa. 1:22, 25 with Ezek. 22:17ff.). It is to Jeremiah most of all that he is indebted. The two share a common understanding of Babylon as the instrument of God's punishment, a hostility toward relations with Egypt, a conviction that the future of Israel lay with the exiles, and a hope for an inner transformation of the people of God. Ezekiel uses Jeremiah's prophecy as a reservoir of ideas (compare Jer. 15:16 with Ezek. 2:8ff.; Jer. 6:17 with Ezek. 33:1–9). This closeness to Jeremiah is not surprising, for Ezekiel undoubtedly followed Jeremiah's career during his youth in Jerusalem.

THE CHARACTER OF HIS SPEECH

The form and fashion of Ezekiel's prophecy are highly distinctive. The reader notices the difference from the earlier prophets immediately. The entire book is constructed by employing the same first-person pattern for reporting the reception of revelations. The clarity and consistency of the pattern makes the units easy to discern and distinguish. The units ordinarily open with the formula "The word of the Lord came to . . ."; Ezekiel is addressed by the title "son of man"; he is given introductory instructions about the message; and the message is introduced by the messenger-formula "This is what the Lord has said." The reports of the reception of messages or instructions about things to be done are usually not followed by any statement that the words were spoken or the deeds done. The reports are written in an expansive and detailed style that is often rhythmic but seldom poetry of a kind heard from Isaiah and Jeremiah. The effect of the whole is autobiographical, though the subject is never the person apart from his prophetic role. The entire book is an account of what the Lord said to Ezekiel. The style suggests that we may think of Ezekiel as one who composed very carefully the revelations which came to him. Perhaps the circumstances of the early exilic community in the early years of the exile offered no ready public platform for public delivery of the revelations. He would draft in his basic form the experiences of divine communication and relate them to those who gathered at his house or came to inquire of him.

Like the other prophets, Ezekiel employed a wide variety of types of speech to communicate his message. There are three which play a major role in his prophecy: vision-reports, symbolic actions, and speeches which develop images or metaphors. All three kinds of material appear in the books of prophets who preceded him, but in Ezekiel they are more frequent and undergo an elaborate development which carries them beyond any previous formulations.

Four vision-reports stand at crucial places in the book as though intended to lend structure and meaning to the whole. In 1:1—3:15, the introduction to the book, the glory of the Lord appears to Ezekiel in Tel-abib, and he is commissioned to serve as a prophet to the exiles. In chapters 8—11 Ezekiel is transported to the temple in Jerusalem to survey the abominations which defile it; while there, he sees the glory of the Lord depart. Chapters 40—48 at the conclusion are a counterpart in which Ezekiel is taken again to Jerusalem to behold the new temple of the future to which the glory of the Lord will return. In 37:1–14 Ezekiel is set in a valley of dry bones and commanded to call them to new life by the word of the Lord, the pivotal experience on which his hopes for Israel were based. In each of these visions the hand of the Lord comes upon him, the ordinary world is dissolved, and he is placed by the Spirit in a scene created by God to behold an inner reality behind the scenery of normal experience. He becomes involved in what he sees participating dramatically in the vision himself. What he experiences in these visions is obviously fundamental to the rest of his prophecy.

Divine commands to perform symbolic acts punctuate the book; there are some twelve in all, a number unmatched in the career of any other prophet (4:1–3, 4–8, 9–17; 5:1–17; 12:1–11, 17–20; 21:11–12, 23–29; 24:1–14, 15–24; 3:22–27 plus 24:25–27 plus 33:21–22; 37:15–28). Symbolic acts are actions performed by a prophet in which an announced event is anticipated in visible drama as though it were already beginning. For example, Ezekiel 4:1—5:17 reports a complex of symbolic acts portraying the fall of Jerusalem. The prophet makes a model of a city under siege, lies immobilized for the number of days equivalent to the years of punishment for God's people, eats the fare of Jerusalem's starving population, and performs signs with his shaven hair which preview what will happen to them. In these acts the person of the prophet becomes instrument of the word, and he himself undergoes the experience of the divine deeds which he announces in his sayings. The degree of participation in the history which God is working out is intense; his own life and body become the sign of God's way with his people.

Ezekiel was a master of metaphors. He is not content, like Jeremiah, to employ figures of speech to lend style and force to his message. He turns the image itself into a long speech in which it becomes the sustained subject, the vehicle through which he delivers the message. Jerusalem is a useless, charred grape vine (chap. 15), an abandoned baby reared by the Lord for his wife (chap. 16). Samaria and Jerusalem are harlotrous sisters (chap. 23). An allegorical narrative about two eagles, a cedar, and a vine refers to the rulers of Egypt and Babylon and to Jehoiachin and Zedekiah (chap. 17). Ezekiel comments on Judah's royal politics with a dirge about a lioness and her cubs (chap. 19). He sings a dirge for a glorious ship to speak of Tyre's fall (chap. 27). Pharaoh becomes a cosmic tree (chap. 31). The speeches verge now on a parable, now on allegory. They provide Ezekiel with a way to restate his basic message of judgment in rich variety.

Taken form by form and feature by feature the prophecy of Ezekiel contains little that is unique. But he is unmistakably different. The difference lies in his capacity to absorb and revive and combine a long inventory of phenomena and elements from priestly and prophetic tradition and to express them in an intense and almost exaggerated manner. In that sense he stands at the culmination of the prophetic succession. His character was appropriate for his task. He was the last of the great prophets of judgment and had to proclaim the final and total punishment of the people of God in a time when the punishment had already begun. It was a mission that called for intensity and exaggeration of all the religious resources of Israel.

THE BOOK

Among all the books of the prophets, Ezekiel's has the clearest and most orderly arrangement. In spite of its length it is relatively easy to grasp the disposition of material in it. Like several other prophetic works, it contains three major parts. Chapters 1—24 contain words of judgment against Israel, the land, and Jerusalem; chapters 25—32 are made up of messages against other nations; and chapters 33—48 are concerned with the future salvation of God's people. The impression which this plan gives of a career that begins with proclamations of judgment and concludes with promises of salvation is largely valid in the case of Ezekiel. The first section is introduced by his call to proclaim woe (1:1—3:15) and the third by the redefinition of his office as the watchman of Israel (33:1–9, anticipated by 3:16–21).

The appearance of carefully arranged material is heightened by a series of dates spread through the book giving the year, month, and day on which certain revelations came to the prophet. There are thirteen in all (1:1; 8:1; 20:1; 26:1; 29:1, 17; 30:20; 31:1; 32:1, 17; 33:21; 40:1; the interval of seven days at 3:16 might be counted also), and they imply that the sayings follow a chronological order. The fact that several dates do not come in exact sequence does not belie the general temporal order of the material.

There is a correspondence between certain units in the first and third parts which gives the two the effect of a balanced relationship. The two call stories have already been mentioned. Judgment is proclaimed to the mountains of Israel in chapter 6 and salvation to the mountains in 36:1–15. The vision of the destruction of the temple and the departure of the glory of the Lord in chapters 8—11 has a counterpart in the vision of a new temple and the return of the glory of the Lord in chapters 40—48. The recitation of the history of Israel's sin in the past (20:1–44; see also chapters 16 and 23) is answered by the announcement of a new salvation history in the future (36:16–38). The second part of the book contains oracles against seven nations, a number that is surely intended to represent completeness. It is set in the interval between the anticipation of the report of Jerusalem's fall (24:25f.) and the reception of the report (33:21f.). This is appropriate since the dates in part two locate the oracles against the nations in the years just before and after the fall of Jerusalem (the date in 29:17 applies to an "up-dating" of an earlier saying).

This carefully planned arrangement, along with the consistent first person style in which the whole is presented, suggests that the book came finished from Ezekiel's hand in its present form. That opinion prevailed through the first quarter of our century. Then a series of studies began to appear which challenged the integrity of the book and the picture of Ezekiel which it gives. One study attributed to Ezekiel only that part of the material which could be shown to be poetry. Another argued that the book is a fictitious work written in the third century B.C. and then extensively revised. Different scenarios for Ezekiel's career were proposed—that he really lived in Jerusalem, that he prophesied both in Jerusalem and then in Babylon, that he began among the exiles and went to Jerusalem and returned. All these proposals are based on aspects of the book itself, but they fail to account adequately for the material as a whole. In recent decades the study of Ezekiel generally takes the book's own portrayal of the prophet and his historical circumstances as a reliable basis for interpretation.

However, the conviction has grown that the book reached its present form by a rather complex process of formation in which others than Ezekiel participated. In the process the prophecy was redacted and rearranged. Only examples of the more important ways in which this took place can be given. (The matter can be pursued by using the commentaries of Zimmerli and Eichrodt). At points the material has been elaborated. The great vision of the Lord in chapter 1 has been enlarged by additions which are interested in the visual aspects of the epiphany (e.g. vv. 15–21 with the description of the wheels). Some original units are expanded by a further development of their subject (e.g. 19:1–9, a lament over kings Jehoahaz and Jehoiakim spoken before the city's fall, is extended in vv. 10–14 by a dirge for Zedekiah which addresses the events of 587). The vision of the new temple has been enlarged by extensive insertions which reflect thinking about the details of its reconstruction (e.g. 40:38–46; 41:5–15; 42:1–14). The collection of oracles against the nations (chap. 25—32) was inserted in an earlier form of the book, interrupting the clear sequence between chapters 24 and 33. A duplicate of Ezekiel's second call (33:1–9) has been attached to the account of his first call (3:16–21).

These few illustrations point to a history of the formation of the book in which both Ezekiel and a "school of disciples" pondered, developed, and arranged his sayings. One can speak of a school because the style and tendency of the elaborations and expansions are clearly dominated by Ezekiel even where the work seems to be done by others. Nothing in the book suggests that work on Ezekiel's prophecy continued beyond the exile. The book must have been completed during the exilic period and brought back to Jerusalem by those who cherished Ezekiel's prophecy as God's word to his people. In a broad sense, then, the whole book is Ezekiel's work.

CHAPTER THREE

THE CALL OF EZEKIEL

In contrast to his older contemporary Jeremiah, Ezekiel rarely speaks of himself. Whatever feelings of frustration and despair he may have felt are kept hidden behind his solemn commitment to speak only of God's word to him. But once a lament breaks forth, disclosing how deeply he was disturbed by the life of an exile. When he was ordered to cook a cake of barley with human dung for fuel, he cried out, "Ah, Lord, I have never defiled myself . . ." (4:14). Even though he heard it from God, the proposal was unthinkable. He was a priest bound to the holy. Uncleanness was dangerous to his person and identity. The lament is a clue to what he must have felt about his exile. He was displaced from holy land and place, condemned to live in an alien, unclean land. Every day and duty of life must have involved offenses to his sensibilities. More than most, a dedicated priest would have suffered in his soul because of exile.

But when the doors of earth were shut against him, the heavens were opened (1:1). He, who thought he was forever banned from the Presence and would never mediate between Presence and people as priest, was transformed into one whose person and proclamation represented God in a wholly unexpected way.

THE VISION

The priest became a prophet. His life, like that of his predecessors, was interrupted by an experience of seeing and hearing which drastically altered his purpose and perspective. The experience is reported in 1:1—3:15. The description of a vision of God is the longest and most detailed in the Old Testament. It is so elaborate and vivid that it became a primary source for the vision literature of Judaism and Christianity.

25

An introduction tells where and when the vision came to him (1:1–3). He was among the exiles by the river Chebar in the land of the Chaldeans. The notice may simply refer to the location of Tel-abib (3:15), but it is possible that the community had established a place on the stream as a site for rituals of lament and cleansing (Ps. 137:1; Acts 16:13) and that the vision came upon Ezekiel in the midst of worship. It was the fifth year of the exile and the thirtieth year (of his life?; the figure is not explained). "The heavens were opened" and "the hand of the Lord" was upon him; both expressions are ways of insisting that the experience happened solely at divine initiative. The vision was not a willful dream, neither was the report an invention of Ezekiel. It all happened to him as realistically as an intrusion upon one's life initiated by someone else. It was an action which God took from his side, an event whose occurrence prepared for Ezekiel's entire prophecy.

The vision is described in 1:4–28. It begins with a storm of cloud and lightning approaching from the north. Amidst the clouds are four man-like living creatures, each having four wings (not named here, but called cherubim in chap. 10) and moving in a square full of flashing fire. They bear a crystal firmament as a platform to support a throne of sapphire on which is seated "a likeness as it were of a human form," its upper part gleaming like bronze and its lower part shining like fire. These are the features of the primary vision. The account pauses at points to dwell on the appearance of the living creatures and the way they moved (vv. 7–11, 14–22, 23–25), elaborations which result from later reflection on the vision by Ezekiel or his school. It is in these reflections that the bizarre and unique elements of the vision occur.

The features of the primary vision have unmistakable connections with older traditions of theophanies and epiphanies in which the Lord of Israel appeared to his people and mediators. What Ezekiel sees is the visual condescension of the God who appeared in the storm of Sinai (Exod. 19), intervened in the thunderstorm to rescue his people (Judg. 5:4f.), and praised as the rider of the cherubim present in the storm (Ps. 18:10ff.). He is the one Micaiah (1 Kings 22:19) and Isaiah (Isa. 6) saw enthroned in heaven, the one who sits above the cherubim on the holy ark (1 Sam. 4:4; 2 Sam. 6:2), the one seen by the elders at Sinai above the platform of skylike sapphire (Exod. 24:10). These recognizable features are not merely catalogued in Ezekiel's vision; they are refracted and merged in a distinctive and dramatic picture of power and intensity. The very accumulation and melding of them creates a complex symbolism through which an overwhelming presence presses on the mind and demands acknowledgment. The way in which the features of the vision are visualized by the imagination of the reader is not as important as the mental and emotional perception of what together they all convey. In spite of its concreteness, Ezekiel's description is not direct. He guards the portrayal repeatedly with language which shows that the elements of the vision mediate someone they cannot fully comprehend. What he sees is the "appearance" or the "likeness" or "the appearance of the likeness." The vision is a way of seeing one whom no one can see (compare the dialectically related statements about seeing God in Exod. 24:10; 33:20, 23; Isa. 6:5; John 1:18; 14:19; 1 Tim. 6:16; 1 John 4:12).

In 1:28 Ezekiel names what he sees, "the glory of Yahweh." The term plays a pivotal role in his prophecy, as it also does in the contemporary priestly account of Israel's beginnings (e.g. Exod. 24:16; 40:34; Num. 14:10; 16:19). In both prophetic and priestly circles the term means the majesty of God's personal presence manifest in shining light. It is not an attribute of God, but the invisible presence made visible. As a priest Ezekiel knows that the place of the manifestation is the Jerusalem temple. His vision of the glory in a distant, unclean land shatters the beliefs that made him feel the honor and power of God were at stake in the fate of the temple. Later in the two temple visions he will see the glory of Yahweh depart (chaps. 8—11) and return (chaps. 40—48), movements that mark off the major phases of his prophecy. Now Ezekiel knows that the Lord means to deal with him outside the temple—and that means not as a priest— with his people away from the temple—and that means not as a holy congregation awaiting atonement.

The import of the vision is as complex as its portrayal. It brings a revelation of God in those aspects of his lordship which address the predicament of prophet and people. God appears in his identity as the lord of Israel's history and worship, the one who intervened in their affairs to save and punish, and was present in their midst at the temple. His coming discloses that the situation of Ezekiel and the exiles has meaning in continuity with that past. He appears also as the cosmic god, free of all limits, sovereign over all of history. It is his dominion, and not the security of his people or the power of

Babylon, that will be vindicated. The whole proclaims to eye and mind above all else—God! What is revealed is that numinous awesome presence of God, radically different from every human being and absolutely sovereign over every earthly power.

The vision is set at the beginning of the prophecy to authenticate the message, to say to the reader that Ezekiel's word is grounded in God. But that purpose concerns us not merely in an external way like some official certification. The vision is recorded so that we may also see it with our imagination and be amazed and struck with awe, may ponder it and respond with mind and emotion. The seeing is there for the sake of hearing the word of God through the prophecy—the very word of God who translates himself into visions that he may approach us. Ezekiel saw, and he fell on his face and listened.

THE COMMISSION

When Ezekiel falls prostrate before the glory, he recognizes that the approach of God is directed at him and waits in the humblest passivity on the divine initiative. God speaks to him in a series of sayings marked at their beginning by the address "son of man" (2:1—3:11). All are components of his installation into the office of a prophet. They are not distinct in theme and function, but are woven out of several motifs which are repeated and represent major aspects of Ezekiel's prophecy. Typically, the whole is composed of reports of what God said. Ezekiel does no more than listen except in the case of that symbolic action in which upon the divine command he eats a scroll (2:8—3:3). He does not even stand up when summoned to rise. The Spirit, which plays such a major role in the movement and experience of Ezekiel, enters him, lifts him up, and gives him the capacity to bear the direct address of God (2:2).

The title "son of man" emphasizes the passivity and humility of Ezekiel's relation to God. It stresses his mortality in contrast to the deity of the Lord. The title is the only way God ever addresses Ezekiel, and he uses it repeatedly. It is not as priest or pious man or Israelite that Ezekiel is called to be a prophet, but as a frail mortal who brings nothing but his weakness to the task. The tension in which Ezekiel is set by the address of the Lord is not that between righteous person and sinner, or between holy and unclean, but the ultimate tension of the naked contrast between God and man. The tension persists throughout Ezekiel's prophecy and finds expression in his self-effacing habit of only reporting the words of the Lord and of submitting his very body to an identification with the message in symbolic actions.

The unifying feature in the long sequence is the repeated word of appointment to be a prophet sent by Yahweh to Israel as a bearer of his words (2:3–5, 7; 3:4f., 10f.). He is to be, like his prophetic predecessors, a messenger through whom the Lord as sovereign communicates with those he rules; the signature of his speech is to be the classic messenger formula "Thus says the Lord." He is to speak only what he hears, and his words are to be the words of the Lord. The instruction to speak "whether they hear or refuse to hear" frees Ezekiel from the burden of responsibility for the reception of his proclamation. It is also a clue to the purpose of his mission. Its success is not dependent on the response of those who hear his words. Once spoken, the words will assume an existence of their own in the midst of Israel. When God fulfills his plans and executes the decisions announced in advance through his messenger, then Israel "will know that there has been a prophet among them." This vindication will show that Ezekiel was indeed sent by the Lord, and what is more important, the correspondence between word and event will demonstrate that what happened was surely the act of the Lord. The prophecy will serve as a "theology" of the events and experiences to come upon Israel and will be a means of understanding the experience of disaster and tragedy as life under the lordship of God. Those who refuse to hear will be pursued by the prophecy until what they see gives them ears to hear.

The character of Ezekiel's message is disclosed in a symbolic action which occurs within the vision (2:8—3:3). A metaphor Jeremiah once used (Jer. 15:16) about eating the words of the Lord takes the form of actual experience for Ezekiel. He is commanded to eat a scroll on which is written "words of lamentation and mourning and woe." His eating represents his obedient acceptance of a message to the exiles that things are going to get worse, not better. He will proclaim words of woe about Israel and its land and holy city until they are fulfilled and his commission is revised. It is this implacable obedience to a cruel mission which the act symbolizes, rather than some kind of verbal inspiration in which all the specific language of his sayings is conveyed to him in advance. The word of the Lord will come to him on particular occasions inspiring and releasing his own potential and resources for expressing the word in words.

Two things are remarkable about the depiction of the Israel to whom Ezekiel is sent. The first is the scope of the Israel with whom he is concerned. His specific audience will be the exiles of his own people, the deported community in Tel-abib (3:11). But his message concerns the house of Israel in its entirety in time and space (2:3; 3:1,4). His words will deal repeatedly with Jerusalem and the population there. He holds the exiles in the context of what is happening at home, insisting that their destiny as Israel is being determined there. Moreover, as he uncovers the sin which invokes God's judgment, he has the whole history of the people in mind; it is not just the present generation, but what "they and their fathers" (2:3) have been and have done which stands at the bar of God.

The second is the extensive portrayal of Israel's consistent corporate sinfulness. God calls them a "rebellious house" (2:5,6,7,8; 3:9), an epithet that will echo again and again in the prophecy; Israel earned the rebuking name because they have a history of not listening to the words of the Lord (3:7). Their failure is a failure to hear and heed, and they will not, God warns, listen to Ezekiel. His mission is, humanly speaking, hopeless and will meet persistent, stubborn rejection. He is to be unafraid and stand them down, face to face, forehead to forehead, matching the hardness of their rebellion with the hardness of his obedience. He is to be among a rebellious people as one who does not rebel, hearing the word of God, in spite of their opposition, for their sake. The unyielding implacability of Ezekiel's prophecy has its origin here. He does not lack passion and compassion; such feelings seeth beneath the surface of his words. But he will be faithful to his commission with a persistent, unflinching obedience that allows his audience only to hear or refuse to hear. In his prophecy he will develop the epithet "rebellious house" into historical analyses of a total depravity unlike anything else in the Old Testament. Ezekiel's call pits him as one man against the whole people in all of their history.

CHAPTER FOUR

WORDS OF WOE

Ezekiel is called by the Lord as divine sovereign to proclaim to the rebellious house of Israel "Thus says the Lord." Exactly what he is to say is not specified. We learn only that he is given "words of lamentation and mourning and woe," that is, announcements of events which will cause expressions of grief and dismay. Under the circumstances, that indirect anticipation to warn of what was to come was sufficient. Where divine lord deals with rebellious subjects, judgment is expected.

So the mantle of the judgment-prophets falls upon Ezekiel's shoulders just when their message neared the climax of realization. One might think that after the humiliation of 597, remorse and repentance would have been in order. But all we know about the population of Judah and Jerusalem indicates this was not their mood. They were still hiding from confrontation with God behind a stubborn misreading of the divine choice of people and city. They clung to the belief that, because Israel was the elect people and Jerusalem was the elect city, no final end would come upon them. Ezekiel's saying in chapter 15 addresses that theological folly. They are, he says, like the wood of the vine, useless for any purpose but to be burned in the fire. And they have already been charred (a reference to 597)! The comparison is a scathing denial that they have any value in themselves which would preserve them from the fire of judgment.

THE ANNOUNCEMENT OF JUDGMENT

The historical course of the judgment announced by Ezekiel can be described quite briefly. Nebuchadnezzar would return to Judah and devastate the land. He would then besiege the city and raze its defenses and temple. No measures of politics or piety could deter the calamity. The attempt to find security by moving under the shelter of Egyptian protection was doomed. Israel's existence as a state would be brought to an end and its population carried away as captives.

But Ezekiel knew this would all happen through revelation of what the Lord had decided. It was not merely a natural, though terrible, sequence of events, but the work of God in which he vindicated the integrity of his reign. So Ezekiel speaks about what is to happen in ways that convey its inner reality and purpose. He renders the coming events in a form which lets those involved experience them as a confrontation with the divine. His speeches make his hearers see the divine fire and divine sword scorching and cutting. He draws them into visions where the heavenly agents of God are executing his wrath. Using symbolic actions, he dramatizes the coming disaster so that it becomes present before it happens. His speeches on metaphors burn the message into mind and imagination.

Early in his career Ezekiel acted out, on divine command, the fall of Jerusalem in three symbolic performances. First he built a representation of a city under siege. After he had drawn a plan of a city on a large clay brick, he set around it all the structures and implements used by armies of the time to assault a walled city (4:1–3). He restricted his diet to the meager rations of bread and water that would be available to a population on the point of starvation because they were shut up in the city. The bread was cooked with dried dung to represent the lack of wood (4:9–17). Then he shaved himself with a sword symbolizing the victory of the foe, divided the hair into three parts, and burned one part on the brick, chopped up one part with the sword around the brick, and then scattered the third to the wind —all this to portray the fate of the captured population (5:1–2). When he had finished, he delivered a divine oracle beginning, "This is Jerusalem which I set in the midst of the nations, with countries round about her" (5:5). The Lord himself had become the foe ("Behold I, even I, am against you," v. 8) of the very city he had made the center of the earth to represent him in the world. When that city no longer stands for the Lord, it has no reason for existence.

During the years before Jerusalem fell, Ezekiel performed one such symbolic act after another. He lay immobilized for the number of days equivalent to the years of punishment of the remnant of Israel (4:4–8). He gathered a few possessions in the kind of pitiful pack captives carry away into exile, and day by day he went out before his fellows as if departing (12:1–7). He ate his daily fare in fear and trembling to point to a population living through days of terror (12:17–20). He drew a map showing two roads for the king of Babylon and put sign posts on them pointing to Rabbah in Ammon and to Jerusalem, the two principal cities in the revolt of 589. When Ezekiel's wife died while the siege of Jerusalem was in progress, he refused to perform the rites of mourning; his conduct at the loss of "the delight of his eyes" was a symbol of the way in which the exiles would have to bear the destruction of the delight of their eyes, the sanctuary in Jerusalem (24:15–24). God made Ezekiel "a sign for the house of Israel" (12:7). The drama of judgment was played out in his person. He was given to a people who did not have the eyes to see or ears to hear what God was doing so that they might have the word before them in living flesh.

What Ezekiel saw in his first temple vision (chaps. 8—11) struck at the heart of Israel's existence. From it he learned that judgment begins at the house of the Lord (9:6 and 1 Pet. 4:17). Only one year after his call, the elders of Israel were sitting before him, apparently having come seeking a word, perhaps about what would happen in Jerusalem. He is gripped by the ecstasy of inspiration, enters the world of vision, and is transported by the Spirit to the temple in Jerusalem. There God shows him four cases of pagan practices in the precincts of the temple, all involving the cults of alien deities. He learns what is believed about the Lord when he hears elders say, "The Lord does not see us; the Lord has forsaken the land." His divine guide repeatedly asks the indignant question "Son of man, do you see what they are doing, the great abominations . . . ?" Then executioners are summoned and sent out to their grisly work, preceded by a priestly figure who marks the foreheads of all who are grieved at the abominations so that they may be spared. The executioners begin at the sanctuary and move out with grim dispatch. At God's order, the priestly figure takes divine fire from between the cherubim and goes out to strew it across the city in an exploding conflagration. With that, the glory of the Lord moves away to the east. The vision ends and Ezekiel tells the exiles what he had seen.

The effect of the vision is stunning. It shows a degradation of religion that is total, a wrath of God that is inexorable, and a judgment that is comprehensive. A fullness of guilt is matched by a fullness of wrath. At one point Ezekiel cries out lest any remnant of Israel be totally lost in the judgment, only to hear the reply "I will have no pity" (9:8–10). What the prophet sees is tantamount to the death of a cult, a city, and a people. There is no future—unless there be a resurrection (chap. 37 is demanded).

Grasping the gravity of the vision depends on knowing what the temple meant in Israel's faith. It was the place where the Lord had chosen to be present, graciously making it possible for his people to be near him and to form their lives around and before him. It was the center that created the congregation, the focus of the relation to God. The depth of Israel's depravity lay in the fact that in the very temple they practiced a worship of which the Lord was not the reality. The offense was more serious than dabbling in other religions. In the place where he was present they found it necessary and desirable to devote themselves to other gods who promised to bestow the security and prosperity the Lord denied them. They took that denial, not for divine discipline and not as a dialogue with them, but as the weakness and absence of God. And so other powers must be worshiped in order to maintain their questions and needs, while the people themselves stand as the central reality in relation to the divine. Ezekiel's vision is the prophetic attack on the perennial proclivity for making liturgy a litany of self and world instead of a response to the clearly perceived reality of the Lord. The departure of the glory is the symbol that the gracious nearness of God is not a submission to selfish perversions of his relationship to man or to insulting presumptions against his Presence, but an offer to allow people to live under his sovereignty.

Until the siege of Jerusalem was under way, Ezekiel proclaimed "the end" for the land and its capital (chap. 6). His commission forced him to deprive the pitiful remnant of exiles of their last tangible basis for hope. He scorned all speculations that the disaster could be delayed or avoided (12:21–28). Even the righteousness of legendary saints would not suffice to protect the city (14:12–23).

THE BASIS OF JUDGMENT

Ezekiel's proclamation of judgment is accompanied by the most comprehensive characterization of Israel's sinfulness in the Old Testament. Prophetic words of judgment had always included a citation of the wrong which merited the punishment of God. But in a quite new way the indictment for sin takes on a certain independence in Ezekiel's prophecy and becomes a subject for extended reflection.

The term he prefers to use from Israel's rich vocabulary of sin is the Hebrew word usually translated "abomination." It frequently appears as a kind of summary concept at the beginning of his discourses on Israel's failure (e.g., 16:2; 20:4; 22:2) and punctuates all his sayings (forty-three times in all). Its role as a comprehensive category in Ezekiel's theology shows his profound perception of what sin means and the deadly seriousness with which he treats it. An "abomination" is a deed or thing that is abhorred because it is totally alien to the character of a group or a person. As a theological term it defines sin as deeds which are inimical to the being of God, as acts which are essentially incompatible with the identity of the Lord. They contaminate and profane his presence and relationships. The term makes it clear that Ezekiel does not think of sin in simple legalistic or moralistic ways as the infraction of rules which are external and incidental to the nature of God. Sin is a calling into question and a contamination of God's nearness and openness to man. It is an assertion from the human side that the Lord is different from his revelation of himself, that he is something other than he really is.

The comprehensiveness of Ezekiel's indictment can be seen in passages like 22:1–16 where the prophet is bid to declare to Jerusalem all her abominations. He carries out the assignment by reciting a list of violated commandments (vv. 6–12) which were given Israel to distinguish between the righteous and unrighteous (cf. Lev. 18). The list is not merely a bill of particular transgressions to be considered in isolation. It has an accumulative force which builds a description of a people deeply involved in "shedding blood and making idols," the kinds of actions which the being of the Lord excludes. The recitation ends with the final interpretative accusation, "and you have (in all these ways) forgotten me." This absence of the recognition of the Lord from such a broad span of activity is the inner truth of Israel's failure. In 22:23–31 Ezekiel lists the classes of society who have profaned the land—officials, priests, prophets, and ordinary citizens—all belong to the guilty. No section of society can say of another, "They are the ones to blame." All have come short of the glory of the Lord.

Ezekiel's accusation takes up the entire history of Israel throughout all time. His prophetic predecessors could look back on earlier times as a period when things were right between Israel and its God (Hos. 2:15; Jer. 2:2; Isa. 1:21, 26). But Ezekiel ferrets out every evidence of perversity and rebellion in the tradition to show that

Israel and Jerusalem were corrupt from the start. God's way with his people has been a story of dealing with sinners from the beginning. Their sinfulness was in a real sense "original."

Chapter 20:1–31 is an example of the way Ezekiel translates the classic salvation-history into a sin-history. Some of the elders in the community come to him seeking a word from God about their situation. God rejects the request and commands Ezekiel instead to judge them by letting them know "the abominations of the fathers," a phrase that can serve as a title for the review of Israel's history which Ezekiel then delivers. The story is narrated in three phases, Egypt (vv. 5–9), wilderness (vv. 10–17), and the second generation in the wilderness (vv. 18–26). Each phase is described on the same pattern: God's provision for Israel's relation to him, their rebellion, and the response of God.

The theological center of the story is its assertion that the norm by which Israel is judged lies in the purpose of God to be known as the Lord. He chose them as his elect people, bound himself to them by oath, promised to bring them to a land of blessing. He gave them his statutes and ordinances as a provision for life and his Sabbath as a sign that he had set them apart to be different from the other nations. He offered the second generation a second chance after their fathers had failed. The divine purpose in all this was to make himself known in and through Israel. He attached his name to this concrete people and took the risk of letting his identity be represented in their career. That is why the urgent summons to reject any involvement with the religion of other people accompanies the election. Use of idols and alien cults was not merely the transgression of one law among others. It was the corruption of the knowledge of the Lord, the defilement of his name, the obscuring of his identity. This holds true for faithfulness to the statutes and ordinances and to the sabbaths. Rebellion was not simply an episode of disobedience; it endangered God himself in his revelation in the world, distorted the announcement through Israel that "I am the Lord."

That is why each report of Israel's rejection of the divine initiative begins with the basic interpretative sentence, "But they rebelled against me." Ezekiel sees all the particular failures as an offense against the divine person. The same theological principle is used to explain why the Lord persevered with such a recalcitrant people. It was "for the sake of my name" that God endured the repeated rejections. If he had poured his wrath upon them in the midst of the nations, he would have profaned his own name in their sight. The theology uncovers the predicament and peril into which election and revelation of himself to willful people brings the Lord. It is this faithfulness to his own purpose in the world that has maintained the history of sinfulness and sustained his long suffering.

The third rejection by the children shows that the problem is endemic. The promise of the land and the revelation of the law and the call to repentance cannot reach the heart of Israel. Before the land is reached, God swears to scatter Israel among the nations whom they want so much to be like that they cannot represent the Lord among the nations (cf. 20:32). Here the theological history reaches across the centuries and touches the events of Ezekiel's time. That is the word to the elders. God had already decided before Israel settled in the promised land to end their history in exile and dissolution. The sin of the first two generations was so great it had confirmed what their descendants would be like, and the word of judgment was spoken over them before the judges and David even appeared. So the story breaks off with the second wilderness generation; it need go no further to answer the elder's questions about their future.

At the conclusion of the story something mysterious and ominous is said through Ezekiel (20:25f.). Israel was given commandments which were not good so that the law which was a means to life became an occasion for death. The bad commandments are the requirements for the dedication of the first born to the Lord (Exod. 13:2; 22:29; 34:19f.). Israel had always understood that the requirement was to be met through the sacrifice of an animal as substitute. But several times during the history of the monarchy, kings had offered up their sons (2 Kings 16:3; 21:6). Ezekiel is saying that the sin of Israel was so total and the decree of judgment so final that God used the law itself to shut the nation up to sin, to harden their hearts against him, and to bring out into the open in the most undeniable and hideous way that they were indeed a rebellious house. So when Ezekiel charges the elders with defiling themselves in the manner of their fathers (20:30f.), he is not referring to something they have individually done, but rather he is accusing them of the history of sin that began in Egypt and ran through the entire career of the people.

Two other theological narratives are used to expatiate on the congenital sinfulness of Israel. Chapter 16 is a story about a foundling born of an Amorite father and a Hittite mother whom the Lord rescued, preserved, and married, only to discover that his bride was an incurable harlot. The use of marriage as an image for the relationship between God and Israel appears in Hosea and Jeremiah. In Ezekiel the image is spun out in the tapestry of an ornate tale told to declare the abominations of Jerusalem, the fatal fascination of alien cults and foreign alliances which drew its populace to unfaithfulness. Chapter 23 is a near allegory about the two sisters, Oholah and Oholibah, representing Samaria and Jerusalem, who become harlots in Egypt. The Lord married them, but they practiced harlotry with gusto, giving themselves away to every male who passed by. Both stories speak of a sinfulness of Israel that is indigenous to the corporate nature of the people and expresses itself as a constant quest for satisfaction and security among the cults and powers of the nations. Something in them resists the Lord and the vocation to be people of the Lord.

The depth and dimension of Ezekiel's doctrine of sin is based at least in part on the fact that he stands at the end of Israel's national history and views it in the perspective afforded by his distance from the daily difficulties and struggles taking place in Judah. Freed from preoccupying confrontation with the demands of the present, he could look back to the beginning and speak of the long course of Israel's life. He uncovered in the whole way of Israel the basis for the climactic outpouring of wrath. It was his calling to disqualify everything in that long past as a basis for belief that there was something in Israel's history or character that justified them in the slightest measure before the judgment of God. The election and the promise of the land and the law had only succeeded in revealing their sinfulness. Now all that was left was the primeval purpose of God that he, the Lord, be known.

That is the purpose which God is pursuing in the judgment announced through Ezekiel. Repeatedly his sayings reach their climax and conclusion with the sentence, "You/they shall know that I am Yahweh" (e.g. 6:7, 14; 7:4, 9, 27; in all, about seventy-two times). The constant repetition of this fixed expression as a statement of the outcome of God's acts shows that it expresses his ultimate purpose. Because they are foretold by prophets and stand in continuity with past revelations of the Lord, the imminent terrible events will be occasions of recognition and acknowledgment. Judgment will accomplish more than the punishment of the rebellious and the vindication of God's sovereignty. In it Israel will be confronted with the revelation of God in his identity as Yahweh and be brought to the moment of recognition that they are inescapably and completely in his presence. The identity of Yahweh will be the great unavoidable reality defining their present and qualifying whatever future there may be for them. The end is upon them, and clothed in its dark and frightening shrouds is the Lord. The terror they face is not meaningless fate but the extreme measure of God to establish dialogue.

CHAPTER FIVE

WORDS OF LIFE

On the fifth day of the tenth month of the twelfth year of the exile Ezekiel was unable to speak because the Lord's hand was upon him. A refugee who had escaped from Jerusalem came to him with the news, "The city has fallen." When he heard the direct report that the event toward which his prophecy had persistently pointed for years had at last occurred, Ezekiel's mouth was opened (33:21f.). The concurrence of the return of speech with news that judgment had come upon the house of Israel can be taken as a symbolic event. From that time the prophet, whose face was set like flint against every hope for the future among his people, began to speak words of life. Across the following years Ezekiel delivered the most extensive and systematic prophecy of salvation to be heard from any prophet up to that time.

Once the news of the dimensions of the destruction and death in Jerusalem sank in, the prophet must have been engulfed in a tide of despairing lamentation from his fellow exiles. Only the divine command to refrain from any display of grief as a sign to the community (24:15–27) kept him from being swept up in their outpouring of sorrow. Echoes of their laments lodged in Ezekiel's sayings: "Our bones are dried up, and our hope is lost; we are clean cut off" (37:11; see also 33:10). This plaint, uttered in the typical words of Israel's language of suffering (e.g. Pss. 31:11; 9:19; Job 8:13; Lam. 3:54), is a cry of those who feel emptied of life and deprived of any future. The phrase "our bones are dried up" triggered from the human side a vision which founded the new phase of Ezekiel's prophecy. The report of the vision (37:1–10) and its interpretation (vv. 11–14) make up the best known passage in Ezekiel.

For the third time the power of the Lord gripped him with an experience of being removed from his surroundings under control of the Spirit. He was placed in a broad valley whose surface was carpeted with bones of a great multitude of people, dead so long the bones were very dry. He looked on a panorama of death, a vast jumbled profusion of remains long since picked by vultures and left to bleach in the uncaring sun. It was a terrifying visual rendition of Israel's lament, the psychic confirmation that their words carried the reality of their situation. As Israel, as the people of land and city and temple and history, they were dead. That a scattered remnant was left only provided for a few voices to chant the mortuary rites.

As Ezekiel stood in the valley of death, God addressed him in two ways. First, with a question, "Son of Man, can these bones live?" The question posed the central dilemma of the prophet's vocation at that point in his career. It arises sooner or later for all who are sent to speak for the Lord. What does one do in the face of a community that finds every reason to think itself finished and hopeless? Join them in their submission to death? Or can there be life? It is a question no mortal can answer confidently, and Ezekiel's "O Lord God, you know" is both an admission of human helplessness and a recognition of God whose power is not limited. The deference of the answer is to God himself and not to any belief in a general resurrection of the dead. Such a belief does not seem to have been present in Israel at that time; the tradition only knew that God from whom all life comes reached across the line between life and death on occasion (1 Kings 17:17ff.; 2 Kings 4:31ff.). So when God spoke to Ezekiel a second time and commanded him to prophesy to the dry bones, obedience had to rest alone on God himself, and was already a form of faith in the God "who gives life to the dead and calls into existence the things that do not exist" (Rom. 4:17).

The word given to Ezekiel was a promise of life to the dead, a word that worked a new creation and brought the Spirit. In the vision the word re-created the bodies and summoned breath for them, an event that can be compared to creation itself (cf. Gen. 2:7). The bones reassembled themselves, took on bodies, and received breath. They who were dead lived. The awesome wonder was a symbolical portrayal of what God could and would do for the remnant of Israel. He will bring them forth from the graves of Babylon and return them to the land, where they will live as his people by his Spirit. It is the deed of the "'God who kills and makes alive" (1 Sam. 2:6). The vision of the power of the word of the Lord to bestow life on the dead was the bedrock on which Ezekiel's prophecy of salvation was founded. The final possibility of salvation prophecy lies in the power of God to raise the dead.

The return to the land is the core component of Ezekiel's prophecy of salvation, a motif already introduced in the promise of Israel's resurrection (37:12, 14). But why God would begin again with Israel in the land they had defiled by bloodshed and idolatry and why the life of the rebellious house might be different from its former sinful way is not said. The answer to those questions is given in Ezekiel's promise of "a new exodus" (36:16–32, and the expansion of sayings of judgment in 11:14–21 and 20:32–44).

The theme of 36:16–32 is "not for your sake, O House of Israel but for the sake of my holy name" (vv. 20f., 22f., 32; also 20:44). The theme has two functions. The first is to maintain the validity of the judgment which had brought Israel's life to an end. Israel had lost the land, and with it the possibility of a historical life of its own, because of their sinful history. The future could not rest in their past. In all his proclamation of salvation Ezekiel never gives the exiles any opening for justifying themselves by moving their own character and conduct back into the center of their relation to the Lord.

The second function of the theme is to uncover the one continuity from the past which did establish a theological basis for salvation in the future. It lay in God's faithfulness to his purpose to be known as lord by Israel and the nations (36:20; see the vehement response of God to the idea that the exiles might simply merge with the heathen nations: "As I live . . . I will be king over you," in 20:32f.). The majesty of his person and will must be vindicated. Israel as "the people of the Lord" bore his name. The honor of his identity was at stake in their destiny. As scattered exiles they profaned his holy name. Their plight gave the nations reason to say that the Lord was either powerless in the world, or fickle in his relationships (36:20). The salvation of Israel is a necessity of the purpose of God! He will take them from among the nations and bring them into their own land in a new exodus that will vindicate his name so that "the nations will know I am Yahweh" (v. 23). The way of God's people in judgment and salvation can serve his glory alone.

This exclusive emphasis on God's holy name is consistent with the entire tenor of Ezekiel's prophecy (e.g. 20:9, 14, 22; 39:7,25; 43:7). Considered in isolation it seems a severe and narrow theology that makes no room for human partners, and reads history as an exercise in divine self-assertion. But the majesty of God is the overwhelming reality in Ezekiel's prophecy. From him we hear not one word of God's compassion, love, loyalty, or saving righteousness. The emphasis is Ezekiel's prophetic claim, announced against the background of Israel's sinfulness and in the hour of the end of God's people, that ultimately there can be only one person and will at the center of faith. Salvation does not modify or cancel judgment. Precisely in salvation the majestic lordship of God must prevail against every tendency to justify the sinfulness of man.

The basis of salvation, however, must be held in dialectical relation to the salvation that is promised. Ezekiel expects a salvation which will profoundly affect the character and will of Israel. God himself will deal with Israel's sinfulness, that stubborn persistent obdurancy in the face of his every initiative toward them. He will purify them from their guilt, that is, forgive them (36:25), will replace their rebellious hearts with a new heart and spirit (v. 26). He will re-create Israel by making his spirit dwell in them so that their relationship to him is internal and inseparable from their persons, involving them individually (v. 27). By forgiveness, regeneration, and inspiration, they will become the obedient covenant people for whom life is a life with God.

In this context we hear the theme "new" (also 11:19; 18:31), the distinctive note of the prophets whose setting is the exile (Jer. 31:31–34; Isa. 42:9; 43:19; 48:6). The "new" is their answer to the failures of the past, the quality of God's provision in face of the collapse of the old Israel, old covenant, and old saving history. In all of Ezekiel's pictures of the recapitulation of the exodus and entry into the land the journey is a pilgrimage from sin to holiness. This time the way through the wilderness is a process of transformation of the people themselves. Salvation becomes not only deliverance from external conditions, but also from the sinfulness of the human heart.

In chapter 34 Ezekiel provides another perspective on God's saving work which complements the strict emphasis on the honor of God. Here he takes up the political questions of leadership of the future. Who will unite, guide, and govern Israel so that the people may have a life of justice, prosperity, and peace? No community can endure without a center that holds it together. The question was all the more urgent because the record of Israel's leaders and kings down to Jerusalem's fall gave depressing evidence that their revival and perpetuation would bring just the opposite. It is typical of Ezekiel that this saying begins with a word of judgment on the failures of those who had governed and actually addresses the entire political history of Israel (vv. 1–10).

The saying as a whole is a prophetic composition on "shepherd" as a metaphor for the leader of a community. The use of shepherd as a title to symbolize the responsibilities of divine and human rulers for their people was customary in the ancient Near East from earliest times. In the Old Testament, the Lord is called "shepherd" (Gen. 48:15; 49:24; Pss. 23:1; 80:1) and his deeds for Israel are depicted as the work of a shepherd (e.g. Pss. 28:9; 68:7; Isa. 40:11), but surprisingly no specific human ruler is given the title. Jeremiah begins to use the term for the rulers of Israel as a group to put their failure in relief (Jer. 23:1–4). Ezekiel takes up the image and in this passage develops it into the longest and most eloquent theological treatment of the divine shepherd in the Old Testament.

The rulers of Israel's history are the undershepherds of the Lord's flock, his people. They have fed themselves on the flock instead of feeding them. So God is against them and will take the flock from them. He himself will do the shepherd's work. He will seek the lost, gather the scattered, lead the flock in green pastures and by still waters. He will give them rest in their land and tend the crippled and weak. The picture is infused with all the duties of the ideal shepherd and sustained until there is a depiction of the good shepherd from which all the later theological uses of the metaphor will draw. Through it the Lord appears as the God who is moved by the harrassed and helpless (Matt. 9:36), who seeks and saves the lost (Luke 15), who cares for the flock instead of exploiting them (John 10).

The whole is a metaphorical exposition of the new salvation-history about which Ezekiel speaks elsewhere in other ways. Here the new salvation-history is announced as an answer to the debacle of political history. How the culmination of God's new work will take form within the temporal social history of Israel is not evident. In this context Ezekiel speaks of the one to come, of an undershepherd whom God will put in office to be his servant in tending the flock (34:23f.). God will make David the leader of the covenant people and his role will be a true expression of God's relationship to his people. In this way God will keep his ancient promise to Jesse's son (2 Sam. 7) and provide a way for Israel to exist as the one people of one god under one prince (see Ezek. 37:15–28 and its promise of the reunion of

Judah and Israel under one king, David). The identity and appearance of the coming David is left in mystery. The promise speaks in terms of "who," not of "how." He will be present when an undershepherd appears who fulfills the office.

The Book of Ezekiel is concluded by a long and complex description of the new temple as the visible determinative center of Israel's future life (chaps. 40—48). The description is presented in the form of a vision-report (40:1ff.) which is clearly a counterpart to Ezekiel's vision of the profanation of the old temple and the judgment provoked by it (chaps. 8—11). The important place which the temple would play for the restored people is indicated in other salvation prophecies. The purged and purified remnant will conclude the new exodus with the worship of God on his holy mountain in Israel (20:32–44). The Lord will set his sanctuary in the midst of the reconstituted people and make his dwelling place with them (37:26f.). In his final vision Ezekiel beholds the realization of these promises in the existence of a sanctuary which perfectly represents the holy presence of God with Israel.

Twenty-five years after his exile Ezekiel is transported in the spirit to Israel and set down before a city on a mountain. He is met by a man of gleaming form equipped with tools for measuring, who proceeds in silence to measure every dimension of the ground plan of a temple. As the dimensions are taken it becomes apparent that the plan excludes pagan practices of the past and dissociates the temple area from the royal palace. The mysterious architect speaks only once; when he measures the inner room of the temple, he significantly breaks the silence to say "This is the most holy place" (41:4). His final task is to measure the wall around the temple area which makes "a separation between the holy and the common" (42:20). When the sphere of the holy is marked off and the holy of holies designated, then Ezekiel sees the awesome theophany, the appearance of the glory of the Lord as he has seen it twice before, returning to the temple which God has abandoned (43:1–12 and 11:23). The glory of the Lord fills the temple, and Ezekiel hears a voice from the temple that states the central meaning of the vision: "This is the place of my throne . . . where I will dwell in the midst of the people of Israel forever. And the house of Israel shall no more defile my holy name . . ." (v. 7). Finally, Ezekiel's guide shows him a stream which begins as a trickle from the temple and swells until it is a great stream flowing away to the east, transforming the barren land of Judah into the garden of paradise full of trees with fruit for food and leaves for healing (47:1–12). It is the mythical river that goes forth from the mountain of God to bring life to the world (see Gen. 2:10–14; Pss. 46; 65:10; Joel 3:18; Rev. 22:1; John 7:38).

The report of this vision (40:1–37, 47–49; 41:14; 42:15–20; 43:1–12; 47:1–12) is the basic stratum of chapters 40—48. Most analyses of these chapters agree that the remainder of the material represents elaborations and additions. They contain regulations for worship, duties of Levitical and Zadokite priests, limitations and privileges of the prince, designation of areas around the temple, and a new sacral division of lands to the twelve tribes. The growth of the original report is the work of those who were concerned with the many specific and difficult problems which would arise when Israel returned to its land and had to reconstitute its religious life. They took the description of the temple as a plan for its rebuilding and added their proposals for dealing with many questions the vision did not address. Their contributions give the resultant whole the appearance of a draft of ordinances for the reconstruction of Israel as a religious state, the direction in which the postexilic nation was in fact to move.

But Ezekiel's experience was a prophetic vision. In spite of the precise measurements of the length and breadth of the temple and its courts, the purpose was not to provide a blueprint for builders. The floor plan is meant to be understood in the same way as the movement of the glory of God and the stream flowing from the temple. The reality is symbolic. The vision is the subject for prophetic proclamation (40:4; 43:10). The meticulous measuring of the holy area is the visual objectification of the promise that God would dwell in their midst forever. The miraculous stream is the promise that God's presence will be the source of blessing and healing. The theological center of the vision lies in the announcement of the divine presence and divine demand: the Holy dwells with the people that they may be holy (43:7–10). The later postexilic community would rebuild the temple. Ezekiel's vision bestows in anticipation a sanctity and meaning on that structure which will invest it with intimations of the glory of the Lord. But the promise and demand transcend the structure and, when it is no longer there, the divine commitment will still hold (Rev. 21).

CHAPTER SIX

HOW THEN CAN WE LIVE?

Part three of Ezekiel's book is introduced by a report of a revision of the terms of his call to be a prophet (33:1–20). The location of the report just before the brief account of Ezekiel's learning that Jerusalem had fallen (33:21f.) indicates that this redefinition of office anticipated the distinctly new situation in which his prophetic ministry would be conducted (3:16–21, an abbreviated version of 33:1–20, has been attached to the report of Ezekiel's call as an affirmation that 33:1–20 is a repetition and extension of his original vocation). The fall of Jerusalem, the destruction of the temple, and the new deportation were combined in an overwhelming catastrophe that marked a radical change in the times. Ezekiel no longer faced a community which refused to believe such an end would come for their nation; instead, he dealt with people who did not know what to believe now that the end had come.

Within Israel the cry was heard, "How then can we live?" (33:10). With the land lost and the nation scattered, the foundations of living were removed. There was no longer any home, identity, and tradition to make up a context for thinking and planning, for decisions and commitment, for remembering and hoping. The community began to disintegrate into various expressions of disorientation. The few people left in Judah could see no other meaning in their circumstances than the sordid opportunity to take over deserted property (33:24–29; cf. 11:21). Despair set in among those in exile who accepted the calamity as confirmation of all the prophetic accusations of their unworthiness to be God's people (33:10). In the minds of many, bitterness turned to rancor at God, and they spat out the resentful indictment, "The way of the Lord is not just" (33:17, 20; 18:25, 29). The spiritual malaise was too serious to be answered by Ezekiel's promises of salvation. The exiles were suspended in an interim between judgment and salvation when the gloom of catastrophe was more real than the light of the future. A prophetic word was needed about their present.

In that situation God made Ezekiel "a watchman for the house of Israel." The office of watchman was a traditional role in Israel's society (e.g., 2 Sam. 18:24ff; 2 Kings 9:17ff.) As a metaphor for prophetic work it had immediate currency; Jeremiah had already dubbed the prophets "God's watchmen" (Jer. 6:17). When an attack came the watchman had to give the alarm; if he did not, he was responsible for all who lost their lives. Of course, Ezekiel and the other prophets of judgment had already played that role, delivering God's warning before he brought the sword on the land. But now the office is given a new function in the changed situation. Since the people as a national community no longer exist, Ezekiel is to warn the wicked person to whom God says, "You shall surely die" (v. 8). The quotation is the form in which sentence is announced to those who have incurred the death penalty because of disobedience to specific commandments. The prophet must confront the individual exiles and warn them of the sins in their lives which will bring death upon them. This new assignment clearly puts a strain on the appropriateness of "watchman" as a metaphor for the prophetic task. Already past was the earlier situation in which God brought war upon the corporate people as punishment. But the use of the term does show that, though judgment had come, the Lord still pursues his purpose with the broken fragments of the nation. Because the watchman's warning is still sounded, there is a chance for those who will hear. The doors are not closed on those who live under judgment. Sober and severe though Ezekiel's new mission be, it is nonetheless the provision of a surprising grace.

In 33:1–20 Ezekiel is told what to say as watchman. The instruction is quite similar to chapter 18 where Ezekiel is told how to deal with those who no longer see any place in the present for faith in the Lord. It is from these two sections that we learn how Ezekiel carried out his ministry as watchman in the days after the fall of Jerusalem. The basic word is a call to repentance (33:11b; 18:30b). Heard among the exiles, the summons to repent must have been startling. They, who thought God was done with them and therefore there was nothing for them to do in faith, were confronted with a call to turn to the Lord and to take up life, one by one, under the covenant. In such a context the grace inherent in the proclamation of repentance to sinners shines through. Through the call to repentance Ezekiel ministered to the resignation and cynicism that were gripping the people around him.

Some of the exiles were paralyzed in resignation: "Our transgressions and our sins are upon us, and we waste away because of them; how then can we live?" (33:10). The lament is a cry of despair from folk who experience guilt as a fate from which they cannot escape. For them Ezekiel has a word which discloses what lies in the very heart of God from whom the call to repentance comes, the marvelous word: "I have no pleasure in the death of the wicked, but that the wicked turn from his way and live" (33:11). The possibility of repentance is based within God himself. His pleasure in life keeps the way from wickedness to righteousness open at all times. The Lord is not implacable fate, an inexorable machine of moral retribution. He moves in dialogue and struggle with people toward the coming of his reign. His opposition to sin and his judgment upon sinners is the work of his left hand shepherding all people toward life. He is the God who desires that all be saved (1 Tim. 2:4), and who works in patience "not wishing that any should perish, but that all should reach repentance" (2 Peter 3:9).

Whoever, then, will hear the call to repentance is set free from the past. The call creates a present that is fraught with the possibility of life, a present in which God begins again with each person. No one can rely on his own righteousness and ignore the call. No one is trapped by past sins and prevented from hearing the call (33:12–15). The choice of the purpose of God, righteousness, and the acceptance of the gift of God, life, are bestowed by the call.

Some of the exiles had fallen into alienation from God. They took up a cynical proverb as their motto: "The fathers ate sour grapes, and the children's teeth are set on edge" (18:2; cf. Lam. 5:7). The saying is a wry resentful claim that the present generation suffers for the sins of its parents. The teaching that the sins of the fathers affect descendants to the third generation was an ancient doctrine in Israel (Exod. 20:5; 34:7; Num. 14:18; Deut. 5:9; cf. Jer. 32:18); that the sins of one generation bring woe on their heirs is also a compelling fact of experience. Ezekiel himself had insisted that judgment would come upon the nation because their history had been sinful from its beginning (chaps. 16, 20, 23). But in the mouth of the exiles the proverb was an excuse and an abuse of theology. It clearly claimed that the present generation was not involved in the guilt of Israel. And it turned a partial truth into a total interpretation of the exiles' situation with its pathetic lament that God's way with them was exhaustively defined in punishing them for the sins of the fathers. That could only mean that God's relationship to them was indirect, through previous generations. This abuse of theology easily turned into the accusation: "The way of the Lord is not just" (18:25, 29; 33:17, 20). That bitter conclusion called into question the entire foundation of Israel's faith.

Jeremiah had promised that the proverb would be given up in the future time of salvation (Jer. 31:29), but the word Ezekiel receives prohibits its use in the present (18:3). Against the assumption implicit in the proverb, he asserted that all persons (RSV "souls") stand in direct relationship and responsibility to God (v. 4). God's relationship to previous generations and to the corporate people does not exclude his direct relationship with individuals in the present. This declaration contained nothing radically new to Israel's faith, but the long history of prophetic preaching against the people as a group and the inclusive nature of the punishment that had come created a need for a new emphasis that God's judgment had gathered up everyone in its catastrophe. But now those who faulted God's justice on account of their plight are confronted with a call to repentance which assaults their cynicism in two ways. On the one hand, they are addressed as sinners; their self-serving excuse is rejected. It is their ways, and not those of the Lord, which are out of line (vv. 25, 29). On the other hand, responsibility for their own life and death is thrust upon them. The opportunity to choose righteousness and life silences their accusations and shifts the question of accountability from God back to them.

In expounding the opportunity which God creates by the call to repentance, Ezekiel re-creates a situation familiar to the exiles. He uses the style of the torah for entrance to the temple in which a summary of the covenant law was held up before the worshiper. This torah liturgy was a testimony to the righteousness required of those who came to stand in the presence of the Lord (see Pss. 15, 24). He makes his own selection of commandments to hold up before the exiles as the model of righteousness appropriate for them (18:5–9 and the free repetitions in vv. 10–18). Far from the temple in an alien land he shows that it is possible to be reckoned righteous and to be accepted by God who is the source and giver of a life that is far more than physical existence. The commandments are a guide to life which frees every person for faithfulness. The series which Ezekiel recites is not a fixed list of requirements to be satisfied in a legalistic fashion. It provides a sketch of obedience, a profile of faithfulness to God and fellows. It contains specific commandments because faithfulness can never stop short with mere feeling and belief, but must be enacted. What is at issue is one's way of life, whether a person is turned toward the covenant God or away from him.

The summons to a life of faithfulness to God and neighbor and so to a life that God reckons righteous, is the prophetic answer to the question, how shall we live, what shall we do? The exiles are not left to flounder in a swamp of resignation and resentment without a word from God about the present. Each is called to take up life under the covenant and to live a life that is presented to God, even though the temple is destroyed and judgment has come. Indeed, the call to repent issued after judgment discloses God's ultimate goal in judgment: to bring Israel to the place where his call could reach their hearts and where the people who were not his people could be re-created as the people of God.

For that reason Ezekiel's ministry to the individual exiles does not mean that God abandons his relationship to corporate Israel as his elect people. Repentance is not an event in the soul of a person that isolates and frustrates community in fragmenting individualism. It binds a person to God and neighbor in concrete unity, draws persons to a center outside them that holds. It is the divine strategy for reconstituting the people of God free of every political and geographical and cultic definition.

There is an inner connection between the call to repentance and the future salvation proclaimed by Ezekiel. He announced the promise that God would give his people a new heart and a new spirit (11:19; 36:26). He also puts the call to repentance in the language of promise: "get yourselves a new heart and a new spirit" (18:31). This pairing of promise and command, of indicative and imperative, is Pauline in character (e.g. Gal. 5:25; Phil. 2:12f.). It interprets repentance as a transaction in which both God and man participate. Repentance is divine gift and work to change the persons who respond to God's desire that they should live.

CHAPTER SEVEN

THE CHARACTER OF THE PROPHECY

In chapters 40—55 of the Book of Isaiah there is prophecy of remarkable power and beauty. The sayings collected in these chapters are the words of a herald of salvation. He announces that the period of punishment for sin is over. Forgiveness closes the door on the past. A new time is dawning which will bring things no one expected. There will be a new exodus. The advent of Yahweh is at hand. A way will be prepared through the wilderness for God and people. God will return to Zion bringing them with him. No difficulty or foe can hinder the return. Zion will be restored, its scattered population gathered to live in peace, prosperity, and joy. The hearers are bid to live in eager hope, to see and understand through the eyes of faith what is happening in the world, and to rejoice as though their redemption had already occurred. They are called the servant of Yahweh because their salvation will show that they belong to him. Their redemption will be a revelation to all humanity that Yahweh is God alone and that all nations live under his power. He will use the servant vocation to bring all the world to acknowledge his gracious reign. There is nothing else in the Old Testament quite like this prophecy for visionary breadth, poetic achievement, and bold hope.

The prophecy has an amazing presence beyond these chapters. In reading them one comes upon place after place where a resonance with texts known from the New Testament is heard and where associations with moments in liturgy and praise arise. The prophecy is strewn with them. "A voice cries: In the wilderness prepare the way of the Lord" (40:3). "He will feed his flock like a shepherd" (v. 11). "Behold my servant . . . my chosen, in whom my soul delights" (42:1). ". . . every knee shall bow, every tongue swear . . ." (45:23). "Behold, the Lord God helps me; who will declare me guilty?"

(50:9). "All we like sheep have gone astray . . ." (53:6). "Seek the LORD while he may be found . . ." (55:6). Such a brief selection suggests the congruence between prophecy and gospel, between prophet and evangelist. And it is only a sample.

Lines of relationship run not only forward to New Testament and church, but even more clearly into the Old Testament history of faith behind the prophecy. It gathers up and throws into a new synthesis many great themes of Old Testament theology. Creation becomes an element of prophetic proclamation (40:12ff.). The covenant with Noah is invoked as analogy for a new relationship between God and people (54:9f.). Hearers are called to "look to Abraham your father, and to Sarah who bore you" (51:2). The promise to the fathers is renewed (44:1–5). It is the God who overthrew horse and chariot in the sea who comes to save (43:16f.). God's people will be provided with water on the way through the wilderness (41:17–20). The relationship between God and Zion will be renewed (52:7–10). The preaching of the prophets of judgment furnishes the interpretation of the travail of the hearers (42:18–25), and the fulfillment of prophecy provides the basis for recasting the first commandment as the proclamation that Yahweh is God alone (43:8–13).

The prophecy, it seems, gathers up the meaning of the past, rearticulates it for the present, and opens up the near and distant future. It is the intersection of what has been and what will be. One important way to study the prophecy is to go through it, marking and reflecting on the points touched by the lines from the past and the future. Nowhere else do we read with such a sense of the canon of scriptures. But one must take care that the actuality and meaning of this remarkable prophecy not be blurred in the wash of associations, but rather that with their own vitality, they define and enrich what has been and what will be. It must be read first for the sake of its own message and its own place in the canon.

Investigation of the meaning and purpose of the material in chapters 40—55 inevitably raises a question about its relation to the rest of the Book of Isaiah. These chapters possess a distinctiveness over against the rest of the book and a coherence within themselves which sets them apart. The most obvious fact about them is that these chapters are a virtually uninterrupted block of salvation-prophecy in the broadest sense of that term. The prophecy reaches a climax in the promise of the restoration of Jeruasalem. Contrast that with the message of Isaiah in chapters 1—39, where that prophet concentrated on the announcement of judgment hanging over Judah and Jerusalem. There is also a difference in literary style which careful readers easily notice. The poetry of Second Isaiah is of an expansive, exhuberant, lyric quality; while that of First Isaiah consists of brief, crisp, pointed rhythmic sayings.

Sensitive interpreters have always observed the change that sets in with chapter 40. John Calvin in his commentary on Isaiah said that here "the prophet" turns to posterity to provide comfort for a people who will be humbled by future calamities. He was quite clear about the distinctive character and purpose of these chapters. By the second half of the eighteenth century, historical study of Isaiah had reached the conclusion that chapters 40—66 were the work of a prophet who lived in the time to which the prophecy was addressed, the exilic period. A century later chapters 56—66 were separated and assigned to the early postexilic period. This critical position has gained steadily as the best way to understand the distinctive coherence of chapters 40—55.

LINES OF AGREEMENT

Today there is broad agreement among biblical scholars about the more important elements of this position: 1) the historical setting of the prophecy, 2) the locale and audience of the prophet, 3) the arrangement of the material into a coherent corpus of sayings, 4) and the distinction between chapters 40—55 and 56—66.

1) The historical setting assumed by the prophecy is the latter part of the exilic period. The correlation between features of the sayings and the circumstances of that time are convincing (consult Chapter One). Jerusalem is spoken of as a captive city, laid waste, and without any significant population; its temple no longer stands (44:26–28; 45:13; 51:3; 52:2, 9). The foreign foe under whose power the Judeans live is Babylonia, who has dealt with them harshly (chap. 47, especially v. 6; 43:14; 48:14; cf. 46:1f.). The exploits of a Persian king, Cyrus, fill the horizon and threaten Babylon; his rise is celebrated in 44:25–28; 45:1–7, and his achievements are reflected in 41:2, 25; 43:13; 46:11; 48:14f.

All these references point to the third quarter of the sixth century B.C. Cyrus acquired an international reputation when he gained control of the Median Empire in 550 B.C. By 538 B.C. he had conquered

Babylon and issued a royal edict which permitted the exiles to return. The return is constantly anticipated in the sayings, but nowhere is there an indication that Babylon had fallen and the return had begun. So 550 and 538 B.C. probably mark off the period of the prophecy.

2) The locale of the prophecy is Babylon, and it is addressed to the exiles who live there (42:22; 43:14; 45:13; 48:20). They are "a people robbed and plundered . . . trapped in holes and hidden in prisons" (42:22). They are weary and in despair, buffeted by the overwhelming currents of history and awed by the gods of their captors. There is no mention of a king or of leaders, no sign of an independent political existence. The judgment announced by the eighth and seventh century prophets is behind them; they still need to understand it, but it is past history and they suffer from its effects. The purpose of the sayings is the exposition of "comfort." The future offered is deliverance—departure ("exodus") from Babylon and return to Jerusalem. Jerusalem will be rebuilt along with the cities of Judah; the temple will be restored. This portrayal of the audience and of their present and future begins in chapter 40 and continues through 55. A few scholars have argued that the locale is Jerusalem because of the sayings addressed to that city (e.g. 40:2, 9; 49:14; 51:17; 52:1). But this phenomenon is best understood as a feature of the dramatic style of the prophecy and its emphasis on the special relationships between God and Zion. Though we are not told where the prophet speaks, the sayings make best sense as messages to the exiles.

3) The arrangement of the material into a collection which shows signs of an ordered plan for a complete corpus distinguishes chapters 40—55 from their literary context. There are introductory (40:1–8) and concluding units (55:6–13); the prologue, like an overture, states major themes which reappear in the body of the prophecy; the epilogue echoes the declaration of the prologue that the word of Yahweh is enduring and powerful. The audience is addressed as Jacob/Israel in chapters 40—48 (the prologue is an intentional exception) and as Zion/Jerusalem in chapters 49—55, the emphasis shifting from the exiles' identity as Israel to their identity with Jerusalem as the corpus moves to its conclusion. Two chapters (54—55), which describe the condition of salvation, conclude the main body (40—53), where the saving action of God is the primary focus. At the center of the main body stands a complex of units (44:24—

47:15) in which Cyrus, Babylon, and the gods of Babylon are expressly named after being spoken of only in general and indefinite references in the chapters leading to the complex, an ordering which creates an effect of climax. Certain units are set at strategic places in the corpus. Two corresponding sayings which deal with the herald who foreruns the return of Yahweh to Jerusalem are located just after the prologue (40:9–11) and at the end of the main body (52:7–10) just before the climactic summons to the exiles to depart. Units of praise are set within the main body as dividers between sections (42:10–13; 44:23; 45:8; 48:20f.; 49:13; 51:3), like the doxologies in the Book of Psalms. The arrangement of the whole is certainly clear enough to indicate that chapters 40—55 were collected as an independent corpus before it was set within the Book of Isaiah. The plan has suffered some dislocation through the insertion of additional material, but it suits the content of the sayings and displays them so well, that the ordering must have been the work of the prophet who composed the material.

4) The separation of chapters 56—66 from 40—55 is based on the different historical settings and audiences implied and the changed subject and purpose of the material. In chapters 55—66 there are numerous indications that the community is in Jerusalem in the postexilic period. The temple has been rebuilt. The sayings speak of the problems which belong to the struggles of the Jewish religious community during the restoration—matters like keeping the Sabbath, the place of eunuchs and foreigners, internal strife. The dangers which threaten are now inside the community. Because the style and themes of chapters 40—55 reappear in chapters 60—62, some scholars have contended that some or all of the material was composed by the prophet of chapters 40—55. A more likely explanation is that this similar material is the work of disciples of the prophet of chapters 40—55 or of prophets strongly influenced by him.

UNSETTLED QUESTIONS

The prophecy in Isaiah 40—55 poses other major questions about which there is no general agreement. Several issues are especially important because the interpreter of these chapters inevitably faces them: 1) the literary character of the material, 2) the unity of the prophecy, and 3) the assessment of the so-called "Servant Songs."

1) The fundamental issue raised by the question about the charac-

ter of the material is whether it consists of short units or long poems. Did it originate as relatively brief sayings comparable to the oracles of the eighth and seventh century prophets? Or was it composed as longer complex poems which combine a number of units or strophes into an original whole? Another form of the same problem is the question whether the material was spoken to an audience or disseminated as writing. We are confronted by the issue when we try to determine the correct limits of a passage for interpretation, or turn to the current commentaries for help in the task. Among the better works on the prophecy there is no unanimity on the question. One seeks to define the smallest identifiable units and finds fifty; another recognizes the existence of several longer poems and finds thirty; a third divides the material into twenty-one long poems arranged in a planned sequence. If we set aside the question of the long poems and seek the smallest complete unit (or strophe), difficulty still remains. Both commentaries and English versions divide the material in different ways. For instance, in chapter 41 RSV separates verse 1 and groups together verses 2–4 and verses 5–7. One commentator unites verses 1–4 and verses 5–7, while yet another merges verses 1–5. And so on.

The difficulty derives both from the way the material was composed and the way it was arranged in the present corpus. The prophecy is the work of a creative person who lived in a period when the distinctness and power of older forms of speech were breaking down and new ones emerging. Many influences and traditions are refracted and reshaped in his sayings. Form-critical analysis can detect many instances of particular types of speech composed as independent units for oral delivery. But this prophet is capable of consolidating several types in a long unit which employs them in combination. The original units, short and long, have been skillfully arranged in sequences held together by catchwords, themes, and a degree of sequential coherence. If it is indeed the case that the prophet created the basic arrangement (though not the final shape) of the corpus, then careful attention must be given to the smallest definable units and to the literary context in which they are intentionally embedded. The uncertainty here does present problems, but wrestling with them will enrich the understanding of the material.

2) The question of the unity of the material in chapters 40—55, whether all of it was composed by the same person, continues to be

discussed. Most scholars attribute the mass of the material to one prophet. One is on firm ground when individual passages are interpreted in terms of the assumptions which hold for the entire corpus. However, there are bits and pieces which may have been inserted, and therefore should be understood in the context of the redaction of the material rather than in the context of the career of the prophet who composed and perhaps arranged the prophecy. It would be surprising if this were not the case, since all prophetic tradition in the Old Testament was supplemented by those who preserved it as a way of interpreting and applying it. A primary theme of this prophecy is the assertion that Yahweh alone is God and a rejection of the reality of other gods. A stratum of polemic against idols (40:19f.; 41:6f.; 42:17; 44:9–20; 45:16f.; 46:5–8) has been attached to the theme to state its obvious implication. It has been argued that the corpus was extensively revised and expanded by a prophet who composed chapters 56—66, but few have agreed that those chapters are the work of one person. Others find brief insertions, which reflect the time and concerns of the period and community to which chapters 56—66 belong, in occasional denunciations, woes, and rebukes in chapters 40—55 (e.g. 44:21, additions to 48; 45:9f.; 50:10f.; 51:1– 8). A word ought to be said here also about chapters 34 and 35. Though separated from the corpus by the narratives in chapters 36— 39, they are in style and theme closer to chapters 40—66 than to the rest of the Book of Isaiah. They probably derive from the same circles responsible for chapters 56—66, but how they came to be in their present location remains a mystery.

3) Without question the issue which has drawn the most intense discussion is the mysterious character of the figure portrayed in 42:1–4; 49:1–6; 50:4–9; and 52:13—53:12. These texts are the so-called Servant Songs because of the title, Servant of Yahweh, given to the figure. Strictly speaking, they are not songs at all. In them a servant is described, a servant with a vocation to bring the nations of the world into a relationship with Yahweh which involves him in suffering to fulfill it. These texts stand in the midst of others which use the same title for the corporate audience of the prophecy in announcing their salvation. In the latter texts the servant is saved; in the former he is used in the salvation of others. The "songs" have been set into the arrangement of the corpus after it had been given its first form. Because of the variation in the roles of the servant and the

secondary relation of the songs to the collection, questions arise. Of whom do the songs speak? Did they belong in the original prophecy? In part the problem of the Servant Songs is also a question of the unity of the prophecy. But the problem is much broader than that. The theology of the servant role, with all it involves, is so crucial in understanding the prophecy that it will be the subject of Chapter Eleven.

A concluding word about the character of the prophecy in chapters 40—55. If it belongs to the third quarter of the sixth century B.C. and is addressed to exiles in Babylon, what of its relation to the book of which it is a part? It does belong to the Book of Isaiah, and that is a feature of its character. We cannot say just how it came to be incorporated in the book; too little is known of the history of the book's formation. But there are clues to why it found a place in the book. There is a certain continuity between the prophecy collected in chapters 1—39 and that in 40—55. For instance, "the Holy One of Israel," which is a specialty of Isaiah as a title for God, is also a favorite of the prophet of chapters 40—55. Both interpret the history of their time as a crisis created by God's use of the dominant great power as the agent of his reign. Both believe that Jerusalem is the crucial medium of Yahweh's relationship to his people and to the nations. Both see that Yahweh is working to create in Israel a people whose corporate life will be a confession that they live in the city of God. Because of such connections, some speak of a "school of Isaiah," continuing generations of disciples who treasured and culti-vated Isaiah's prophecy and suggest that chapters 40—55 is the work of one who stood in that tradition (cf. Isa. 8:16). It is possible. In any case the book in its final form is a massive record of classical prophecy in and about Jerusalem from its beginning in the eighth century to its conclusion in the postexilic period. The origin of the whole was the impulse of the great Isaiah's prophecy. In its final form it is a witness that the word of the Lord endures and works its pur-pose. That witness, heard at the very beginning of chapters 40—55 (40:8), may well be a sign of the real continuity which binds the book into a theological unity.

CHAPTER EIGHT

THE PROPHET

Prophecy requires a prophet. Behind the distinctive coherent corpus in Isaiah 40—55 stands a messenger of Yahweh who composed its sayings. But his own name and story are hidden. The corpus contains no reports about its author, as do many of the other prophetic collections, nor does it supply evidence with which to reconstruct even a sketch of his career. When the corpus was incorporated into the Book of Isaiah any traces of his identity vanished. Yet we have to name him and speak about him. Everything learned from the study of Old Testament prophecy argues that prophecy was addressed to the time and circumstances presupposed by the speaker. It was not, as prophecy, spoken for the benefit of future audiences—that is its later canonical role. It was spoken to its audience about their future, and made them see the present in the light of the future. So a prophet with a mission to the exiles in Babylon must be assumed. He is usually designated "Second Isaiah" because of the book in which his sayings stand. The name is only an awkward contrivance, but we shall use it because to employ another designation would only lead to confusion.

In spite of the mystery surrounding his identity and career, it is possible to conclude some things about his prophetic work which are useful in its interpretation: how he became a prophet, the manner of his speaking, and something about his relationship to his audience.

THE VOCATION OF SECOND ISAIAH

Chapters 40—55 do not contain a report of a prophet's call like the ones in Isaiah 6, Jeremiah 1, and Ezekiel 1—3. Yet 40:1–8 portrays an event in which the transactions of vocation occur. God's new policy is announced (vv. 1–2); a strategy for its execution is ordered

(vv. 3–5); and a person is recruited and commissioned to declare the plan to those it concerns (vv. 6–8). The expected narrative framework is absent; we are not told where the scene is set or who is speaking. The passage unfolds as a series of proclamations by unidentified voices. In verses 6–8 someone is confronted with the order to serve as herald. He protests against the commission, but his protest is overcome. This sequence of commission, protest, and overriding answer is a typical structure of the call story. Verse 6 contains the only reference by Second Isaiah to himself in the first person (so the versions; the Hebrew text has third person). This once, where he reports how he became a prophet, he speaks directly of himself.

The style and content suggest that the setting of the scene is the heavenly throne room where Yahweh is holding court to determine and ordain what is to be done on earth to actualize his dominion (see 1 Kings 22:19–28; Ps. 82; Isa. 6). The voices belong to beings who fill the heavenly royal court and serve as mediators between God and the world. Like Isaiah of Jerusalem, who was brought by vision and audition into the divine council, Second Isaiah is drawn into the heavenly court and made a messenger to announce its decisions. Here the visionary dimension drops away; all occurs as pure audition, as an event of the word of Yahweh. The beginning is a command of "your God" concerning "my people"; another manifestation of the coming reign of Yahweh, which takes the form of God's way with his people in history, is about to occur.

Set at the beginning of the corpus, 40:1–8 serves two purposes. Like the call reports in other prophetic books, it furnishes a validation of the following prophecy. In these verses Second Isaiah asserts that his role and message came from divine initiative, they were thrust upon him. What he prophesies originates in an encounter with God, not in his own will and thinking. His proclamation is a sign of the coming reign of God. An introduction to the following corpus is provided in 40:1–8. Its subjects and themes anticipate what will be heard in his sayings. A careful and thorough reading of the passage will uncover lines that lead out to the structural elements of the rest of the prophecy. The foundations of Second Isaiah's proclamation are laid in the experience reflected in this text.

The call wrought a fundamental change in the life of the person it grasped. His protest against the command to proclaim disclosed the condition of his soul (40:6b–7). The protest takes the form of a lament at the transience of human life and loyalty (cf. Job. 14:1ff.; Pss. 90:5–6; 103:13ff.). It expresses despairing resignation to the unending failure and death that fills his experience, the only pattern of things exiles could see. He could believe that God's power was behind the pattern, but nowhere found ground for confident hope. In this he was at one with his fellow exiles whose own laments will echo frequently in his prophecy. The answer given his lament is the assertion that the word of Yahweh is what endures, is what gives continuity and meaning to life, and strength to loyalty. Look only at the human predicament and there is no reason to prophesy. But remember what the word of the Lord has wrought, and yet can—in that recognition there is reason enough.

The corpus is arranged so that its first word is the command of the Lord to "Comfort my people." This opening testifies to the basis and origin of the prophecy. In all its forms the final purpose of Second Isaiah's proclamation is to obey the command. In his vocabulary "comfort" means more than sympathy to sooth misery; comfort is the strong word of help which bears the relieving, redemptive reality in its language and allows the soul to lay hold on the help in anticipation. Second Isaiah becomes the consummate prophet of salvation. Like the great prophets who preceded him he knows that he stands on a line between the times (v. 2). But they stood in the crisis when the past history of salvation was changing to judgment, while he finds himself in the moment when judgment gives way to salvation, the moment when the forgiveness of God replaces the sin of the people as the basis for his way with them (cf. 43:25; 44:22). The excited, exalted awareness that a new era in God's history with the world is dawning will reverberate throughout Second Isaiah's prophecy. "Behold, the former things have come to pass, and new things I now declare . . ." (42:9).

The heart of his message is given him in hearing that "the way of Yahweh" is being prepared in the wilderness (vv. 3–5). Advent is at hand. The "way" is a double symbol for the meaning of advent. It invokes the power and purpose of the classical salvation-history of the exodus from Egypt. The way in the wilderness is the way God brings his people from the bondage of the world's powers to freedom under his reign. That "event" is about to recur in a new exodus. The way also refers to the royal sacred road that was a feature of the plan for the great Mesopotamian temple-cities; it led through the gates to the temple-palace in the heart of the city. King and images of gods passed along it in ritual processions; pageants were performed to show where the real power in the world resided. But a highway for the Lord (not Babylon's gods) through the wilderness (not into the city of Babylon) is a powerful form of polemic. Yahweh will enact his own pageant of power which all mankind can see. The revelation of the preparation of a way through the wilderness gave Second Isaiah his two major themes: the new drama of salvation and Yahweh as God alone.

By his call, then, Second Isaiah, became a prophet whose vocation was to anticipate the advent of Yahweh as king and savior of Israel, and of the whole world. He marked a new era based on forgiveness, proclaimed the kingdom of God, and brought good news of salvation. He has sometimes been called the evangelist of the Old Testament. With good reason! In 41:27 God speaks of "a herald of good tidings" he has given to Jerusalem. In 52:7 the herald proclaims peace and salvation by announcing the reign of God. In the Old Testament "the herald of good tidings" is the messenger who is sent from the field when the battle is won to bring the news to those whom the victory saves. The Greek Old Testament translates the title "evangelist." It is not an inappropriate title for a prophet with a vocation like that of Second Isaiah.

THE LANGUAGE OF THE PROPHET

In carrying out his commission to comfort God's people, Second Isaiah used a variety of types of speech that were traditional in Israel's culture. Most had been employed by the prophets before him. In this and other ways, he clearly stands in the prophetic succession. Like them he spoke in divine first person style (e.g. 41:1ff.) and marked sayings as messages with "This is what Yahweh has said . . ." (e.g. 43:1). He also spoke his own words to his audience (e.g. 40:27ff.).

His basic message is appropriately expressed in salvation-oracles at whose heart is the statement that God turns to his people and intervenes on their behalf. The salvation-oracles are cast in two varying forms which have been called promises and proclamations. Both in customary use were designed as responses to laments. The first belonged to a cultic setting and was the response of a priest to a prayer of distress by an individual. With it the priest assured the one in need that God had turned to the person and acted to provide relief.

Second Isaiah adopted the type for address to the corporate exilic community, speaking personally to them as if to an individual (41:8–10, 14–16; 43:1–4, 5–7; 44:1–5). The proclamation of salvation was the customary type with which a prophet answered a lament of the community in times of trouble. It usually cites or alludes to a cry of need and then announces the way God will intervene to deliver the community (41:17–20; 42:14–17; 43:16–21; 49:7–12). It is in this basic stratum of his prophecy that Second Isaiah appears as the consummate prophet of salvation and confronts his audience as a community for whom the cry of need is the only religious language left them.

Another major group of sayings is formed as trial speeches. They are oracles which use the roles and vocabulary of legal proceedings to create an imaginary setting in a judicial court. Second Isaiah uses the type in two ways to overcome resistance to his message of salvation. One group of trial speeches portrays a suit of Yahweh against nations and their gods, which he brings to prove that he alone rules history and therefore is God alone (41:1–5, 21–29; 43:8–15; 44:6–8 plus 21–22; 45:20–25). One of the purposes is to persuade the exiles that nothing could hinder the help of the Lord. In the other group of trial speeches Israel is summoned into court to settle the validity of their complaints against the Lord because he let them suffer humiliation (42:18–25; 43:22–28; 50:1–3). Their grievances against God alienated them from their one source of help and had to be dealt with if they were to hear the proclamation of salvation.

Second Isaiah composed dispute speeches, sayings in which an argument is advanced against a mood or opinion held by his audience (40:12–31; 42:18–25; 45:9–13; 49:14–26; 51:17–23). In these also the prophet struggles with the soul of the exilic community. Here the focus is on the theological and personal morale of the exiles, the erosion of their faith, and sense of identity.

The language of the Psalter had a special influence on Second Isaiah that is unique among the prophets. Types, styles, and themes which belong to Israel's worship are woven into his sayings in a variety of ways. Brief hymns, which summon Israel and the cosmos to rejoice because of the Lord's advent, punctuate the collection (42:10–13; 44:23; 45:8; 48:20f.; 49:13; 52:9f.; 54:1f.). These hymns are prophetic in character because they celebrate the event Second Isaiah promises as if it were already present. They are invitations to rejoice in the present because the future is already grasped in faith. The hymnic style of describing God in a series of "the one who . . ." sentences is frequently employed to emphasize the identity of Yahweh (e.g. 43:16f.; 45:24–28). Subjects like the praise of Yahweh as creator of the world and ruler of history, and patterns such as the juxtaposition of the majesty and mercy of God, all characteristic of the Psalms, are employed to give theological substance to the prophecy (40:11–31 is a parade example). The laments, so often taken up in the proclamations of salvation, disputations, and trial speeches, belong of course to the psalmic category.

Along with these more frequent types, a number of others are employed for particular purposes like the royal oracle to Cyrus (44: 24—45:7), the taunt-song against Babylon (47), instruction to a herald of good tidings (40:9–11). The Servant Songs offer examples of yet four more forms. The numerous types are sometimes used individually, but often they are merged and varied to compose longer units (e.g. 51:9—52:3; 41:8–13).

The presence of psalmic influence in the prophecy is so unusual that it suggests the prophet belonged to a circle who remembered and cultivated hymns and prayers in exile as a way of keeping faith and identity alive. They would have been a minority, because the general audience reflected in the prophecy shows little signs of such devotion. But it may have been from such a core group that Second Isaiah received his basic nurture in Israel's faith. His command of the style and substance of hymns and laments is remarkable. Perhaps it was also in this milieu that his extraordinary talent as a poet was stimulated and trained.

THE AUDIENCE

Second Isaiah's commission created, humanly speaking, an impossible situation for him and his audience. It was comparable in many ways to that situation created by the mission of Moses for him and the Israelites. The exiles were a captive fragment of a small shattered nation living a precarious marginal existence under the shadow of the greatest state on earth. The prophet was to announce that history would rearrange itself to provide for their future (incredible), that Babylon was through and its gods nothing (subversion). At best such talk could stir up false hopes; at worst it could invite reprisals.

Taken as a whole, the Jewish exiles were not a promising congregation. Nothing in their circumstances and little in their consciousness reinforced the message. Their mood would have been no better than the prophet's, who at the time of his call could find no other pattern in the flow of things than failure and death. They were a people whose past was filled by a massive calamity that blotted out everything before it. If they believed the prophets of judgment, that disaster was divine punishment, they were left to live with the wrath of God or his absence. Decades had passed since their exile began, and time seemed to confirm their fate; life would have to go on as it was. There was no way to make peace with their miserable lot and hold to their traditions and faith. Either God was not "our god" any longer, or not really the god at all. They were exiles not only from their land, but also from their god.

The theological achievements of some individuals in the exilic community demonstrate that there were exceptions to this resignation. Yet the dismal picture is a fair profile of those whose spiritual state is reflected in the prophecy of Second Isaiah. Their anguish shapes his address and their laments can be heard in his sayings. God had rejected and deserted them (49:14; 50:1). In spite of their cultic devotion to him, He had given over to destruction (43:22–24) and left them in the hands of spoilers and robbers (42:22). Zion had no future (49:21). They could not be delivered from their captors (49:24). Their destiny had passed beyond the control of the Lord (40:27).

The fashion of his prophecy shows the intensity of the prophet's engagement with the plight and plaint of his audience. The oracles of salvation answer their laments. The disputations struggle with their discouragement. The trial speeches attack their anxiety about the powers controlling their life and their grievances against God.

The prophecy has a passionately pastoral quality. It is a real speaking to the heart (40:1), a ministry of proclamation that seeks to sustain, persuade, and encourage. Second Isaiah frequently addresses the community as one person. His address builds up their sense of identity as the people of Yahweh by emphasizing their election and God's acts in their behalf in the past. He calls them by a title, previously given only to figures like kings and prophets, "the servant of the Lord," which means one who belongs to the Lord, one who is protected and represents him. The title is a way of saying to them that the honor and purpose of God is at stake in the question of their destiny. (A good illustration of those features of the prophet's address is found in 41:8ff.).

Second Isaiah undertook to reverse the exiles' way of thinking, to change their minds about what is real and possible, to bring about a kind of repentance and conversion. They were thinking of God in terms of their predicament and anxiety; he sought to make them think of their situation in terms of the reality of God (55:6, 8f.). The disputation in 40:12–31, for instance, tries so to place the exiles in the presence of the greatness of God that they can receive the strength that comes to those who wait for the Lord. God's deliverance moved the early Israelites from lamentation (Exod. 2:23; 3:7, 9; 14:10ff.) to praise (15:1ff.); this prophet seeks to take away the laments of the exiles and put hymns on their lips before they cross their own "Red Sea" (41:16; 43:7, 21; 51:11; 54:1). He wanted them to see now what he saw, to perceive that in the storm of their time the Lord was working their salvation (42:18, 23; 43:10, 19).

But it was no easy task. We do not know how many received his message and beheld his vision. There were surely some, because the material in chapters 56—66 at places reflects his influence on thinking about faith and life after the return from exile. But in his own time the prophet had to call his audience "blind and deaf" because they did not hear and could not see what the Lord was doing for them (42:16, 18f.; 43:8). There was particular resistance to his announcement that the Persian King Cyrus was Yahweh's anointed (45:1 and 45:9–13). What he suffered from his own people and from the Babylonians is hidden in the mystery about his career. But it may be that his mission involved him in the penultimate scene of the passion play formed by the prophetic succession of those who proclaim the kingdom of God.

CHAPTER NINE

THE PROCLAMATION OF SALVATION

The proclamation of Second Isaiah is easy to describe in terms of its historical reference. If we ask what he announced and reduce the question to one of bare external events, the answer can be found in the oracles about Cyrus in 44:24—45:13. Second Isaiah expected the Persian to overthrow the political structures of the Near East and to vanquish Babylon in the process. He would free the Jewish exiles to return to Judah and provide for the reconstruction of Jerusalem, the rebuilding of its temple, and the restoration of the cities of Judah (44:24, 28; 45:1, 7, 13).

To reduce his proclamation to historical facts is to distort it. But it does throw into relief the crucially important fact that like the other canonical prophets Second Isaiah was dealing with the actual flow of international history. It was a basic ingredient of his prophetic discourse, the sphere in which he wanted his audience to experience and understand the reality of God. It was their very real historical predicament with all its impossibilities which he addressed, and it was the disruptive change breaking upon the region and shifting all situations toward new possibilities that he wanted his hearers to see. He did not offer them a solution to be sought in their own subjectivity or promise a solution beyond time and space. His proclamation called for the kind of attitude and insights and decisions which belong to social and political existence in this world.

This is not to say that the prophet was an astute observer of affairs who simply saw through what was happening with unequaled clarity and courage. The foundations of his understanding and anticipation were not laid in attentiveness to events and calculation of their outcome, but in the voices he had heard speaking in the divine council. Because he knew the way was being prepared for the advent of

Yahweh, he looked about him to see how this could be. But he did look to history to see, so essential was the prophetic conviction that the God of Israel works out his way with men through history.

Of course, he did not speak as a "historian" or about the bare facts or mere "historical" possibilities. His vocation was not to help the exiles think through the probabilities of history, but to summon them to live up to the possibilities being created in history by the coming of their God. His proclamation about what was happening took two closely related forms. The first was the announcement that Cyrus is the agent of Yahweh and instrument of his purpose. The second was the portrayal of Yahweh's advent in the world, his way through the wilderness, and return to Jerusalem as a drama of salvation into which the exiles will be drawn. The two are somewhat different ways of talking about one sequence of events. The first shows the relation between what was happening in history and the purpose of God. The second portrays what was happening in history as the deed of God.

GOD'S WORK IN CYRUS

The fullest form of the announcement about Cyrus is found in the pair of sayings, 44:24–28; 45:1–7 and the following disputation, 45:9–13. Cyrus is also the subject of 41:1–5 and referred to in 41:25; 46:11; 48:14f.

The general purpose of Second Isaiah's sayings about Cyrus is the disclosure that his career is the work of Yahweh as creator, lord of history and God of Israel. These three identities of Yahweh are related dialectically to the phenomenon of Cyrus in Second Isaiah's prophecy. The relationship is particularly apparent in Yahweh's self-description in 44:24ff. Because Yahweh is creator, he governs what happens in the world and therefore must be behind the achievements of Cyrus. Because Cyrus' career fulfills the purpose of Yahweh as Israel's God, he, Yahweh, must be lord of history and the only God. The prophet thinks in both ways, giving emphasis to first one perspective and then the other. It is impossible to assign one or the other priority. In his call he came to know that Yahweh's advent was imminent, and in the faith that Yahweh works in history he looks about in the world for the manifestation of that history-changing event—and sees the history-changing work of Cyrus. His confidence in the Lord's election of Israel and Zion lets him see in the career of Cyrus the opening into the future where the promises and prophecies given

Israel in Yahweh's name may be fulfilled. So Cyrus is the place in history to which he points in proclaiming the turn of the ages from old to new.

Without any doubt Cyrus was the overwhelming event of the time. Due to his strategy, campaigns, and policies the structures of power in the Near East were being dissembled. He was viewed as a threat in every quarter. The reign of no king and the borders of no people were secure. The rapidity of his rise heightened international anxiety. The alarms could have only increased the distress and apprehensions of the exiles. Already a victim of the imperialism of the great states and having lost all that gave history any meaning for them, they were about to be swept up in yet one more dissolving maelstrom of struggle over power in which little flotsam of national groups like the Judeans were tossed about and lost. In the midst of the turmoil one of their own stands forth and points in precisely the direction from which the new threat is coming and announces "our God is doing this." He offered them history once again as a sphere for living in faith. That he pointed to Cyrus belongs to his time. But his declaration that the crises of history are not empty of purpose is prophecy for all who believe that the creator is their God and lord of history.

The vision that a great state which was shaping history was the agent of Yahweh was, of course, not unique. In Isaiah's time, Assyria was "the rod of Yahweh's anger" (Isa. 10:5), and for Jeremiah and Ezekiel Babylon was the instrument of divine wrath. What is different and new in the Cyrus-prophecy of Second Isaiah is the focus on an individual foreign king and the role assigned him. Yahweh says of Cyrus "He is my shepherd" (44:28) and speaks to him as "his anointed" (45:1)! The designations are surprising and revealing. The titles are closely related. "Shepherd" is a title frequently given rulers in the ancient Near East to connote their relationship to the people over whom they are set, usually by a deity (see above, pp. 43f.). "The anointed" (in Hebrew *māšîaḥ*, transliterated in Greek *messias*, translated *christos,* English "messiah-christ") identified the king as sacral, as the one selected by God for his office. Heretofore, it had been the title of kings of Judah. It referred, not to the relationship between king and people, but between God and king. And it did not yet refer to an eschatological figure of the end-times. A Davidic king of Judah as Yahweh's messiah was the official who provided protection, prosperity, and justice as expressions of Yahweh's reign (Pss. 20, 72) and represented Yahweh's claim in the midst of the nations of earth (Ps. 2). The designation of Cyrus by these titles meant that he had been chosen by Yahweh to assume the office once given to the Davidic kings. When Jerusalem fell to Babylon, the kingship of the Davidides was broken and ended. Now the office reappears; once again a prophet designates the Messiah—but he is the Persian Cyrus! It is Cyrus whose victories in this time benefit Israel as God's people (45:4). It is Cyrus who, as David once did, shall provide for the building of Jerusalem (44:26, 28).

The theological implications are tremendous. It means that God had detached the messianic office from the Davidides and bestowed it upon one whom he could use in this new situation "to fulfill all my purpose" (44:28). Cyrus' messianic vocation was to "build my city" and "set my exiles free" (45:13). Henceforth, the title would belong to him whose career served the presence of God and the people of God in his time. Second Isaiah saw no future for the Davidic kingship; the one place where he mentions the old covenant with David, its promises are transferred to the people Israel (55:1–5). The designation also means that Israel's role as the chosen people had been depoliticized. Their vocation would no longer take the form of a national state, but the form of a servant (45:4; see the discussion of Israel as servant below). It would not be through the politics of power but rather through obedience to another kind of corporate destiny, to another kind of existence as a community that Israel would itself serve the purpose of God.

THE ADVENT OF THE LORD

The second scenario of events in Second Isaiah's proclamation is a drama of salvation in which Yahweh is directly the actor and into which Israel is gathered as participant. Yahweh would work through Cyrus to create the opening in history for the drama, but Cyrus' role as the anointed involved a relationship with Yahweh, not with Israel. What will happen to Israel as salvation is portrayed as a theophany, as an appearance of Yahweh in history, a marvelous processional through the wilderness, and a triumphant return to his city. The basis for this scenario is the heavenly command which the prophet heard in the experience of his call that a way through the wilderness be prepared for Yahweh. The scenario as announcement is his central proclamation of comfort to Yahweh's people because the divine intervention will overcome their distress; they will be led in safety through the wilderness and will be brought to Jerusalem as the booty gained by their triumphant God. The drama issues in promises of a new life in Jerusalem where growth and prosperity and security will be theirs. The proclamation, then, includes both the action of salvation and its result, the condition of salvation.

All the acts of the drama do not appear in any one of the prophet's oracles. Various sayings focus on different episodes and combinations of them. Yahweh will intervene in the hopeless situation, going forth as the divine warrior as he did in the days of Israel's beginning (41:13ff.; 51:9f.), and will overcome all the enemies and problems that oppress and distress his people (41:8–13; 43:3–4, 14; 47:1–15; 49:24–26; 51:12–15). They will go forth from Babylon (48:20; 52:11f.). They will accompany Yahweh through the wilderness where he will provide for all their needs (41:17–20; 42:16; 43:19–21; 48:21)). He will return to Zion, bringing them with him (40:9–11; 51:11; 52:7–10).

In their life in Zion they will enjoy the benefits of salvation. The city will be restored to an unparalleled magnificence and its people will live in faithfulness, prosperity, and security; the blessing of God will rest richly upon them (44:1–5; 49:16–21; 54:11–17). The population will burgeon; all the offspring of Zion scattered to earth's corners will be gathered home (43:4–7; 49:18; 49:22–26). They will live in an everlasting covenant of peace (54:4–10, 15–17). The nations of the world, their former threat and problem, will turn to them in respect and hope, recognizing in their salvation the power and presence of the one, true God (45:14–25; 55:1–5).

These two foci of the proclamation are evident in the arrangement of the sayings. Chapters 41—48 present the saving action, and oracles on the outcome of salvation appear primarily in chapters 49—55. The two sectors also reflect the place of two major theological traditions in Second Isaiah's proclamation. In the first, the language and motifs of the exodus are taken up and given new expression. In the second, the place of Zion as the city of God comes into play.

The deliverance from Egypt, the wonder at the sea, and the preservation in the wilderness compose the classic picture of Yahweh's saving activity. Through "the exodus" Israel had been formed as a religious community, and they thought of Yahweh as "our god who brought us up out of the land of Egypt." Echoes of exodus are heard repeatedly in the language with which Second Isaiah describes what Yahweh is about to do for the exiles. All the parts of the original are spoken in the announcement of the drama about to occur so that it becomes a recapitulation of Israel's beginnings: the departure from the place of oppression (52:11f.), the miracle at the sea (43:16f.; 51:10), the divine guidance on the way (42:16f.; 48:20f.) and provision for the journey through the wilderness (43:19f.; 49:9f.; 51:11; 55:12f.).

This appropriation of the exodus tradition contributes to the proclamation of the imminent salvation in several related ways. Obviously it gives the message a correlation with the situation of the exiles. Like the early family of Jacob they are held prisoner by the greatest state of the time, forced to spend their lives in its realm and away from the place where they could have an identity and a future. Only an "exodus" out of their historical and geographical alienation could bring them relief, and only the convincing promise of help for the way would give them hope. That God speaks through the prophet's message as the God of exodus re-creates that knowledge of his identity which gives the exiles reason to trust the message. The address of the God of exodus also makes them recall that Yahweh is the God who overcomes great powers, commands the sea, makes water spring in the wilderness. The one who speaks is the one who does such things. By construing the present in the language of exodus, the proclamation puts their time in a perspective that allows those who will hear it in faith to read history's threatening and meaningless turmoil as a new chapter in the history of salvation. It releases the potential always present in faith in a God known through his deeds, the expectation that the intention of those deeds is at work within the storms of the present.

When the proclamation speaks of what lies beyond the journey through the wilderness, the accents of the Zion tradition, whose fullest expression outside prophecy is found in those psalms called "Songs of Zion" (Pss. 46, 48, 76, 87; cf. Ps. 132), are heard. According to the Zion theology Yahweh had chosen Jerusalem for his habitation, the special place of his presence as the king of glory in Israel's midst. It became the historical focus of his divine royalty, a sign to the nations and their rulers, invulnerable to their attack, a channel of the blessings of salvation and joy to his people. All those accents are heard in Second Isaiah's sayings about Zion. Jerusalem is "my city"

(45:13), the holy city (52:1), "graven as the palms of my hands" (49:16). God will make her more magnificent than before, bless her with prosperity and peace, keep her against all threats (54:11–17). The approach of God to Jerusalem is portrayed as the arrival of a victorious king to resume residence in his capitol after his campaigns are complete (40:9–11; 42:7–10), a historical enactment of the old ritual process in which the ark was brought into Jerusalem as the palladium of the King of Glory (cf. Ps. 24). It is remarkable that the theology of the election of David plays no role in all this (see the reassignment of the promise to David to the corporate people in 55:1–5); there will be no messianic regent in Jerusalem as before the exile. Neither is the temple and its cult given an important role. The emphasis is entirely upon God, city, and people. God alone will be directly king and dispenser of blessing. The city will be the sphere of his sole relationship as Savior to his people.

CHAPTER TEN

THE ASSERTION OF GOD

"I am Yahweh, your Holy One, the Creator of Israel, your King" (43:15). The prophecy of Second Isaiah is strewn with sentences like that. They are one sign of a dominant characteristic of his message. He takes up directly and extensively the subject of the identity of God in a fashion unparalleled in other prophetic works. There is an astounding emphasis on the one for whom he speaks, an assertion of God himself, which has the purpose of creating the possibility of hearing and trusting the message. The intention is to re-create in his audience an awareness of the reality of their God. It is particularly in this dimension of his prophecy that the theological work of the prophet is most evident. He is, of course, not a theologian in the philosophical or systematic mode. Yet it is clear that he is drawing broadly on the resources of Israel's tradition of faith, responding to the culture in which he lives, and reformulating and recasting the tradition in a fresh way that corresponds to the questions of his community and the challenges of the period. The presentation of God in his language is one of the creative theological achievements of all times.

The assertion of God takes a variety of forms. There is a virtual catalogue of names and titles of the God of the Old Testament gathered from a variety of periods and settings and distributed in his sayings. The primary list includes: Yahweh, your God, God of Israel, Yahweh of hosts, Holy One of Israel, Mighty One of Jacob, Rock, King (of Jacob), Savior, Redeemer, everlasting God, Creator (of the ends of the earth, etc.). The names and titles are used in various combinations.

Often at the beginning of sayings there is an elaboration of the introduction of the divine speaker. Second Isaiah is not content with the formula, "This is what Yahweh says," but extends the identification by sentences and titles which sustain the accent on the speaker so that the hearers are confronted with references and deeds which bear forth the divine person more fully (e.g. 43:1, 16f.; 44:6). On occasion the prophet will develop descriptions of the God known through Israel's traditions of faith and inquire urgently if his hearers have not heard and do not know who and what their God is (see 40:12–17, 18–24, 25f.). Announcement by God of his own identity and sole divinity penetrate the collection (e.g. 43:11, 15; 44:6b; especially the entire saying 44:24–28). Frequently these devices and formulations are expressions of literary styles, themes, and patterns at home in Israel's hymns of praise (see above, pp. 67f.). The connection is no accident because it was in hymns of praise that Israel was accustomed to confess its faith, to speak of the deeds and character of their God. When these hymns echo through the proclamation of Second Isaiah, the echoes infuse the sayings with that sense of God's reality which language at its best is capable of expressing.

This assertion of God is not dealt with as a separate subject; it is not usually the single concern of one saying. It is woven into the proclamation of the divine drama of salvation and supplies the bedrock of its promise and certainty. The prophet received his call from "your God" and his commission concerned "my people" (40:1). The assertion of the one who speaks through the prophet accents both aspects of the divine identity—that he is *God* and is *yours/ours.* Each aspect is crucial, but they are not kept separate; one flows into and bears on the other. He is God in that he is Creator of all that is and Lord of all that happens. He is "your God" in that he has created Israel for himself and makes events conform to serving Israel's redemption. He can use the world and the nations to produce a new drama of salvation, because he alone is God; and he will, because he is "your God." This dialectical character of the assertion of God grows out of its prophetic intention. It carries out the commission to comfort by confronting the exiles, who had their own despondent sense of themselves and their predicament, with the reality of God, who is the true source of their identity and destiny. The assertion of God is at the same time an offer to them of a restored identity and redemptive future.

YOUR GOD

The identity God had given himself in relationship to Israel is expressed first of all in names and titles associated with many periods and settings in the history of Israel as his people. The very possessive pronouns in "my people," "our/your God" and the title "God of Israel" all connote the relationship established by God's own initiative in his election and salvation of Israel and in his covenant with the people in the days of the fathers and Moses. His personal name is Yahweh (pronounced "Adonai" in the Masoretic text, and usually translated LORD in capital letters in English versions), the name he gave himself as the sign of the deliverance from Egypt (Exod. 3:13ff.; 6:2ff.; 20:2). He is the "Mighty One of Jacob" (Isa. 49:26) who was with the fathers and their families in their wandering toward and in the promised land (cf. Gen. 49:24). He speaks as "Yahweh of hosts" (Isa. 44:6), a title associated with the ark and its symbolism of his leadership through the wilderness and in their struggles with their enemies. He is called "King of Jacob/Israel" (41:21; 43:15; 44:6), a role established in the Sinai covenant and celebrated in the praises of the Jerusalem temple. As divine sovereign over Israel he had provided a reign of guidance, protection, and help manifest especially in defense against foreign enemies. In this way he had gained the name of "Savior" (43:3, 11; 45:15, 21; 47:15; 49:26) because he had been an ever present help in time of trouble, the one who had kept Israel in existence. Frequently, Second Isaiah uses the designation that apparently was created by First Isaiah (6:3), "the Holy One of Israel" (41:14, 16, 20; etc., thirteen times in all). It is the title of Yahweh as distinct from and exalted above all human life, unapproachable in his demanding and judging majesty. Every one of these titles has obvious connotations that are relevant to the predicament of the exiles. Their recitation was an invocation of the one present in all the divine deeds that initiated and shaped Israel's history from the fathers down through the prophets.

Most of all, Second Isaiah spoke of Yahweh as "Redeemer" (participle as title 43:14; 44:6, 24; 47:4; 48:17; 49:7, 26; 54:5, 8; verb 43:1; 44:22, 23; 48:20; 52:9; 51:10). In its ordinary use "redeem" belongs to the social sphere of families and clans and was a term at home in the ethos of kinship. The verb denoted the act of restoring the integrity of a kinsman when it was lost. It was the duty of the near kin to buy back lost family property, to repurchase those who had fallen into bond slavery, and to prosecute blood vengeance. The redeemer was the one obligated to act in this way by the ethos. Second Isaiah did not originate the theological use of the term, but he did raise it to the level of a central theological concept. It fitted his theological purposes ideally because as a symbol it could combine a representation of God's relationship to Israel, his action on behalf of the exiles, and the result of the act all in one expression. Yahweh is proclaimed as the divine kinsman who delivers his own from economic bondage and personal captivity. The restitution of home, freedom, justice, the restoration of the lost integrity of Israel's existence, is his purpose. In a situation in which an Israelite could no longer act as the redeemer of his brother, the captive, homeless, oppressed exiles are told your God will be your Redeemer.

GOD ALONE

Along with the revival of the meaning of "your" there is a coordinate emphasis on "God" in Second Isaiah's prophecy. In the first chapter of the corpus there is a long saying (40:12-31) in which the prophet wrestles verbally with his audience in an effort to create a vital sense of what "god" means as a designation of Yahweh. He returns to the task constantly in the rest of the prophecy. The meaning of "god" was not self-evident in his time, nor is it today. In a polytheistic age one must always specify which deity. And since "god" as a generic term refers to what is not tangible to common experience, the identifying characteristics of what is named "god" are unsettled. Second Isaiah undertook to make the word a symbol which bore the reality of the One who spoke through him and which would waken a faith that was able to trust and respond to his proclamation. "Your God," he said "is Creator of heaven and earth and Lord over all that happens."

Second Isaiah is, of course, not the originator of faith in Yahweh as Creator; it was present in Israel's religion from early times, though never treated as a crucial factor in a sustained way. He can appeal in argument to faith in the Creator as present in his community (40:12-14, 21, 28). But he is the first prophet to take up the theme, and he develops it in a way that makes him one of the primary theologians of creation in the Bible. He unfolds the doctrine to its fullest scope and gives it a new setting. Yahweh by word and act created the heavens and their host and the earth with man upon it (40:12-14, 25f.; 42:5; 44:24; 45:12, 18; 48:13; 51:13, 16). That way of putting it is meant to exhaust all spheres of existence and all beings in them. It leaves no room for other divine beings and powers; the totality of all is distinct from and subordinate to the one. As "God of all time and Creator of all space" (40:28) he is the illimitable in contrast to the finite. This aggressive thrust of creation-faith toward the limits of knowledge and language is a response to the environment of the prophet's mission. His community had lost its home ground and was set in the midst of the whole world, in territory foreign to its experience. Babylonian religious culture adored the stars as mentors of destiny, and commingled the divine with the state and the processes of nature. In response to this different view of reality, Second Isaiah brings out the cosmic and universal potential in Israel's knowledge of Yahweh in a clear and ordered form that is similar to Genesis 1 which was written in the same period and environment.

Creation assumes a new relationship and role in Second Isaiah's prophecy. In other religions creation was correlated with the seasonal cycle and its power was seen in the fertility of nature. In old Israel's faith the Creator was both the source of life and of the blessings which support it and the limit on the aggressive sin of humanity. But in Second Isaiah creation is correlated with the events of history. In his thought creation is not only an act at the beginning of the world, but also the constantly repeated intervention of Yahweh in the course of things. Creation is spoken of not so much to focus attention on the cosmos as on history; history is read as cosmic process and the two are united. A look at most of the contexts in which Second Isaiah speaks of the Creator shows that the purpose is to connect what goes on in the world with the Creator of the world. If Yahweh is Creator, nothing that happens in history can be outside the sphere of his power; history and creation are not to be thought of in isolation (see especially 40:11–31; 44:24–28; 45:9–13; 51:12–16; 54:16f.). The existence of the cosmos and the history of Israel are united under the one rubric "creation," a move which gives Second Isaiah's address to the exiles an unprecedented complexity and depth. The relationship of Israel to Yahweh takes on a cosmic setting; the old history of election is seen as embedded in creation itself. The foundation is laid for portraying salvation as the work of the Creator, as an event which manifests the power of the Creator and expresses his purpose (see 41:20; 45:8; 48:7). The coming salvation is the emergence of the "new," and therefore creation (42:9; 43:19ff.; 48:6). The cosmos participates and responds (41:17–20; 42:11ff.; 44:23; 55:12). In this new salvation God's work against chaos continues (51:9–11; 45:18f.).

The central affirmation of Yahweh as God is made through the proclamation of him as sovereign over all that happens in the world. The emphasis on creation blends into and supports it. As was the case with the creation theme, Second Isaiah is taking an element of Israel's classic faith in Yahweh and both pushing it to its limits and giving it new functions. The conviction that Yahweh controlled the events of history which affected Israel was common to all the prophets. Second Isaiah formulates the conviction totally and exhaustively. Yahweh is the first and the last; history happens within the encompassing reality of his sovereignty; absolutely nothing is outside it. He restates the covenant obligation of Israel to have no other god besides Yahweh. He sees in the record of prophecy before him and in the cogency of his own prophecy the validation of Yahweh's sole godship, the evidence that he alone rules over the affairs of earth.

It is in the two sayings in which Cyrus is named that the theo-logic of the proclamation of Yahweh as lord of history is most clearly stated. The first (44:24–28) claims that Cyrus fits into the continuity of Yahweh's works. It moves through a description of the deeds of Yahweh to a statement of his current purpose, and then incorporates Cyrus as the one through whom his purpose will be fulfilled. Yahweh speaks to Israel as its Creator and Redeemer (v. 24a) and recites his works. He made all things (v. 24b). He contradicts the omens, divinations, and calculations of those who represent the gods and nations (v. 25), while the word of his prophets is confirmed in what happens (v. 26a; read "servants" instead of the singular in RSV). His purpose is the restoration of Jerusalem and Judah, a purpose announced by prophets in the past and by Second Isaiah (v. 26b). He who commands the cosmic deeps (v. 27) now announces that Cyrus is the one through whom his purpose will be carried out (v. 28). The proclamation of Yahweh as the one who created all and who maintains his word in history is the basis for the assurance that what is happening through Cyrus will fulfill the prophecy of the restoration of Jerusalem. The saying moves from the works of Yahweh as God to Cyrus as the deed of Yahweh.

The second saying (45:1–7) is addressed to Cyrus himself. It moves from Cyrus as the deed of Yahweh to the proclamation of Yahweh as God alone. Cyrus is identified as the one whom Yahweh has anointed to overthrow the nations and rulers (v. 1) and to whom he has given the promise that he will be with him in the task (vv. 2–3a). Though Cyrus does not know Yahweh (v. 4b), he will in his triumph serve the universal revelation of Yahweh as the only God (v. 5f.) and continue his purpose for his people (v. 4a). The saying closes with the most daring and disturbing statement of radical monotheism in the Old Testament (v. 7). What is happening through Cyrus is the disclosure of the truth about all events. History is without exception or qualification the expression of the one God. Whether its events appear to be darkness or light, whether they bring disaster or well-being to those who are affected, all is the work of Yahweh whose "creation" history is.

The themes and thinking of faith present in the Cyrus-oracles are used by Second Isaiah in a set of sayings which show that behind the problems of history the question of God is hidden. They are the trial speeches, sayings composed of the acts and roles and language usually employed in legal process of a judicial court (41:1–5, 21–29; 43:8–13; 44:6–8; 45:20–25). As the sayings unfold, plaintiff and defendants are summoned; evidence is called for and presented; witnesses are heard; conclusions are reached and the findings of the court are announced. The process is civil, rather than criminal, one in which issues of rights and prerogatives are being settled. Second Isaiah composed the trial speeches as a way of communicating his prophetic vision of history as a vast judicial proceeding in which the "god question" was being settled. The nations and their gods are summoned because they are the ones whose power and purposes compose history (41:1; 43:9; 45:20). The issue being settled is their right to be gods, to be considered as the shapers of history (41:23). The evidence presented is the crisis created by the career of Cyrus (41:2–4, 25). The argument turns on prophecy: who has shown by prophecy and fulfillment, and particularly by prophecy concerning Cyrus, that the continuity of events is an expression of his power (41:22f., 26; 43:9; 44:7; 45:21a)? The finding is that Yahweh alone can produce a record of purposes announced and fulfilled and has set in the world a herald to announce the fact and future of Cyrus (41:27; 43:10, 12; 44:8; 45:21b). The verdict is that the gods are nothing and Yahweh alone is God (41:24, 28f.; 43:11, 13; 44:8b; 45:21b).

Even at the distance of our own time from the sixth century B.C. these rhetorical trials are startling in their theological courage. In them, Yahweh, the God of a people who live in Babylonian captivity without land, state, or religious establishment, tries the gods of the great states and declares they are worthless and unreal. Yahweh alone is God. What he is defines the word god. He is the only possible subject of a sentence which has god as predicate. Clearly these sayings are the expression of faith; what they portray only a believer could see. Spoken to the exiles they are an attempt to change waning belief into a faith that can see what the prophet sees in the turmoil of the time. The exiles lived in the midst of the pomp and power of Babylonian politics and religion; the images of its gods and pageantry of its rulers were the visible reality that imposed on their consciousness. Their daily experience taught them that the meaning and future of history belonged to this impressively tangible power. It made their eyes blind to the prophet's vision and their ears deaf to his proclamation of salvation.

The persuasive appeal of the Cyrus-oracles and the trial speeches lies primarily in Second Isaiah's argument from prophecy (see the reference to argument from prophecy above). The saying which derides the chief gods of Babylon, Bel (Marduk) and Nebo (Nabu), is another instance of the tactic (chap. 46, see vv. 8 ff.). In Second Isaiah's thinking, prophecy argues for the assertion that Yahweh alone is God in two ways. First, there is the interpretation of Cyrus. The prophet points to the one whose career is a crisis for Babylon and her gods (46:1f.; chap. 47) and greets him as the agent of Yahweh; he shows how Cyrus is working to accomplish the purpose of Yahweh. Because Cyrus fits into the purpose of Yahweh declared by the prophets and is announced by Second Isaiah as Yahweh's herald, the Persian is evidence that Yahweh is God, and the gods of the nations are nothing.

The prophet also points to the prophetic tradition, to the way in which prophecies spoken in Yahweh's name have already been fulfilled in the past. The fact that the prophets of the eighth and seventh centuries had foretold the judgment of Israel and Judah, and that the judgment had occurred in unmistakable and conclusive fashion was one more piece of evidence that Yahweh could and did fulfill his word. In the trial speeches the criterion for deity is the manifest power to make a coherence of events, to shape a continuity by a sequence of correspondences between word and deed. Yahweh has created a history of faithfulness. His word stands forever; it does not return to him empty (40:8; 55:10f.). There is room for only one such divine word in the world of human affairs, and Yahweh has shown that the ultimate word belongs to him. He is the one who makes it possible to live within the sound and fury of history by faith instead of fear or resignation or arrogance.

The trial speeches are more, then, than a mere apologetic aimed at the exiles. They reveal what is afoot in the history of humanity. The basic prophecy about Cyrus and Babylon and Israel was fulfilled. Israel was liberated to live as a community of faith in the midst of the world. The history of faithfulness provides a people who by their prayer and praise testify that the Lord alone is God. The trial speeches indict whatever else mankind turns to in hope of salvation (43:11; 45:20f.); they condemn states which in their arrogance make themselves divine by saying like Babylon, "I am, and there is no one besides me" (47:8, 10).

One of the trial speeches declares that the great trial being conducted in history will issue in a new relationship between Yahweh and the nations (45:20-25). Indeed, the verdict goes against only the gods and the states who dream their power is absolute. But the "refugees of the nations," those who see the powers in which they trusted go under, are invited to "turn to ME and be saved." Because there is one God and one Savior, salvation lies with him. The ultimate purpose of Yahweh in his action through Cyrus is to let the whole world know "there is no other" (45:6) and to bring about the universal confession of his saving sovereignty (45:25). The redemption of the exiles and the recapitulation of the exodus will manifest the glory of Yahweh to all humanity (40:5; 52:10). Then nations and their rulers will acknowledge that God is with Israel (45:14; 49:7, 22f.). The meaning and future of history, they will see, is not in imperial states and patron deities but is borne in the congregation of the faithful who dwell in the city of God.

CHAPTER ELEVEN

THE SERVANT OF YAHWEH

At the human focus of Second Isaiah's message stands the "Servant of Yahweh." The designation already belonged to the vocabulary of Israel's faith, but the way it is used in chapters 40—55 is a unique characteristic of the corpus. For the first time an entire group is called "Servant of the Lord." For the first time the role involves a vocation to suffer vicariously for the sin of the world.

BACKGROUND OF THE TITLE

It is important to understand the designation "servant" in the context of its usage in the Old Testament rather than to assign it a meaning derived for our own experience and culture. The proper antonym is not one who is idle or does not work, but one who is lord. Servant is a relational term whose actuality depends on context. It is not restricted to one status (slave) or to one activity (work); it designates anyone related to a superior (slave, subordinate, vassal, soldier, official, minister). A servant is a person who in some way belongs to another. When the term is used to speak of a relationship to God, the primary sense is belonging to and being kept by, never mere subordination. It is never demeaning but always positive.

In the Old Testament people call themselves "servant of the Lord," or are given the title, in two ways which are particularly significant for its use in Second Isaiah. In prayers of lament spoken by individuals in trouble, those who pray to the Lord name themselves "your servant" as a way of expressing their claim and dependence on God and their hope in him (e.g. Pss. 86:2, 16; 116:16; see 123:2 where the human servant-master relationship of dependence is used as an analogy for the relationship of believers to God). When one is a servant of the Lord, then that person is identified with the Lord who has a vested interest in and concern for what happens to him. It is to his Lord that the servant turns when he is in need.

It is also the case in the Old Testament that God designates a succession of persons as his servant. The title is bestowed on patriarchs, Moses, David and other kings, and prophets as a group. All of them receive the title because they play a role in God's relationship to his people. Here a particular service is in view, a vocation received and performed as agent of God's purpose for Israel.

Both these uses of the title are taken up and given a particular development in chapters 40—55. The entire community of exiles is spoken of by God as "my servant" and addressed as if they were a single believer who had cried out in distress to his Lord. And a servant of the Lord appears whose career serves the purpose of the Lord, not only for Israel, but for the entire world.

THE SERVANT WHO IS SAVED

In the oracles of Second Isaiah, the Lord often calls Israel "my servant" (41:8f.; 42:19; 43:10; 44:1f., 21; 45:4; cf 48:20; the contested 49:3; is dealt with in the next section). The designation of a corporate group by the title is an innovation of the prophet. It reflects laments in which individuals call themselves "your servant" in prayers. By using it as he does, the prophet addresses his hearers as if the people were one person who had cried out in distress to God. Through the title God speaks as if he answers, saying, "I am your Lord, the one you can count on." This individualization of the community is one of the factors which gives the prophecy such a pastoral tone. As a name for Israel "my servant" is not an independent theme of the prophecy. It belongs to the proclamation of salvation and calls the exiles to be those who wait for the Lord and look for his salvation.

This function is reinforced by its reguar association with the idea of election; ". . . whom I have chosen" or "my chosen one" are regular synonyms for "my servant" (41:8f.; 43:10; 44:1f.; 45:4; cf. 42:20; also in 42:1). The notion of Israel's election had been avoided or attacked by the prophets of judgment because it had become a basis for presumption and irresponsibility. But Second Isaiah faced a folk who believed that God had rejected them (49:14; 50:1ff.). His emphasis on election is the response (e.g. 41:9). He understands Israel's election, in dependence on Deuteronomy, as unconditioned choice by God based wholly in his inexplicable love. Israel's status as

servant was established in its election. God named Israel "my servant" when he called Abraham (41:8) and gave the people their
historical existence (44:2, 21). He will save them now solely because
they are his chosen servant.

So, first of all, "my servant" is a word of grace. The status is the
result of God's action; salvation will express its reality. To be the
servant of the Lord is to live in faith that one's future is safe in the
purpose of God.

In two of Second Isaiah's trial speeches (43:8-13; 44:6-8, 21-22)
"Israel my servant" is given a specific role to perform. The speeches
portray judicial proceedings between the Lord and the gods of the
nations to settle the question who is ruler of history, and the decisive
evidence is to be the validity of prophecy. In the course of the trial
the Lord says to his servant Israel, "You are my witnesses" (43:10,
12; 44:8). Though they have been deaf to his words and blind to his
deeds, they were chosen to be the ones who know and believe the
Lord, and understand that he is God alone. The two trial speeches
are in effect a summons to Israel to respond to their election to be
servant by being a community of faith. Simply by acknowledging in
confession the Lord's words and deeds among them, they are his witnesses in the great trial of history. In playing this role the servant
people can be a messenger whom the Lord sends (42:19; the meaning of "his servant/his messengers" in 44:26 is uncertain).

When the exiles are called the elect servant and given the role of
witnesses to the nations, an important shift is being made in God's
relationship to the world. The combination "my servant/my chosen"
had been applied originally to the kings in David's line who represented the Lord's rule to Israel and the nations. When the titles are
bestowed on the community, it means that now Israel will play the
part originally given to David. In fact 55:3-4 explicitly says that the
covenant with David is passed on to the people. God had made him
"a witness to the peoples," but now nations will turn to the people of
God because of his work in and for them.

Even in this specific role of messenger and witness, Israel's service
is a receptive acknowledging response to the words and deeds of God
whose work is the real subject of the witness. The congregation serves
by being saved; they witness by prayers of hope, hymns of praise, by
every way in which they confess faith in the only God. The prophetic
intention of naming Israel the Lord's servant is clear. Second Isaiah

seeks first to recall the exiles to an awareness of the identity created in their election and to assure them of their salvation, and second, to summon them to see in their salvation the answer to the threat to their faith posed by the nations and their gods.

THE SERVANT WHO SAVES

There are four texts in Second Isaiah whose subject is the career of the Servant of the Lord. In them we hear the servant speak and hear him spoken about. We learn of his office, his obedience in suffering, his fate and future. Yet in spite of all we are told, the prophetic intention of these texts is not clear. Their obvious purpose is to point those who hear and read them to the servant, but they give him no identity of which the interpreter can be confident. Therein lies the powerful mystery of these passages.

In 42:1–4, the servant is presented and his commission announced. God is heard speaking. The setting assumed by the style of his speech is the occasion on which a king appoints a minister to represent his rule. God is designating one who will serve in the administration of the kingdom of God. The servant's credentials are the approval and support of God who equips him with the charisma to carry out his task. The servant's commission is stated three times to give it emphasis: to bring God's judgment to the nations, the judgment that the Lord alone is God and therefore the only Savior. The servant is God's representative to set matters right in history, the sphere of his rule, to bring humanity's course from confusion and falsehood, to order and truth. The way the servant is to carry out the assignment is described in negatives: not with forceful words or deeds employed by the ministers of earthly kings is he to bring forth justice. Instead he will offer an instruction for which all people in their essential humanity long.

In 49:1–6 the servant himself speaks to the nations to report how he came to have a commission from the Lord concerning them. The report resembles the call-story of a prophet in many respects; its purpose is to validate the servant's mission to those to whom he is sent. He was, he says, chosen by God before birth, equipped to speak cutting, penetrating words, and supported in his task. His task was to bring Israel back to God and restore its remnant. Though he maintained his confidence in God, his work had been fruitless. Now God has made the astonishing decision to broaden his commission to include the nations! He is to be a light for them, the one through whom salvation comes to all the earth. His faithfulness in failure is the beginning of a mission unlimited by nation and geography. (In 49:3 the servant is identified by the name "Israel," which raises the question how Israel could have a mission to Israel. The most probable explanation is that the name has been added to the verse under the influence of the "Israel, my servant" texts.)

In 50:4–9 the servant (cf. v. 10) speaks again of his vocation and career, this time with the style of a song of confidence. He describes himself as one whom God daily teaches what to say to the weary (cf. 40:30). His message has provoked persecution, but he accepts the suffering as vocation. He persists in obedience, submits himself to his opponents. He confesses that God gives him strength in his travail; though others shame him, he is not ashamed. If God be for him, then who can be against him, for the Lord will vindicate his service and bring the hostility of his enemies to naught.

In 52:13—53:12 the servant is not present. God makes an announcement concerning him (52:13–15 and 53:11b–12), and a group who are not identified directly respond with a report of what the servant has come to mean for them (53:1–11a). God proclaims the servant's achievement and exaltation which, he says, will astonish kings and nations because they are confronted with the completely unexpected vindication of the humiliated servant. Then a group speaking in the first person, presumably representatives of the nations, recounts the change that has come over them through the servant. They had seen no reason in his birth or person or life to think him significant; he was unlikely, unattractive, and unwanted. But now they know that the very suffering which made them avoid and blame him was a service of bearing punishment for their sin, willed by God and accepted by the servant. The servant, they say, suffered in submissive silence, was put to death in obscurity, and buried in shame. But now they confess that it was all the plan of God to atone for their sin. In opaque, yet specific terms, they speak of an existence of the servant beyond his travail, in which he realizes the fulfillment of his vocation for himself and others. At the conclusion God speaks again to declare that the servant will be honored as one who had won a victory because at the cost of himself he stood in the place of sinners.

These four texts place the Servant of the Lord and his vocation in the center of attention; they point us to him and let us listen to him. What does the prophet who composed these passages intend? Who is placed before those for whom they were written? Features of this servant connect him with the exiles in their role as servant and with the prophet himself. Yet other aspects of the portrait resist either identification as an adequate answer to the questions.

The servant passages stand in the midst of sayings in which Israel is named "my servant . . . my chosen," a status they too were given "from the womb" (44:2 and 49:1). The people are personified as an individual who suffers humiliation in captivity and are given a role as witness to the nations. But the figure in our texts is not named (save in the dubious 49:3). He had a mission to Israel from the beginning of his career. His portrayal as an individual is so detailed as to outrun the device of personification and approach the biographical. Unlike "my servant, Israel" he is not deaf and blind, does not lament his suffering or rebuke God. He listens to God, submits to his lot. His vocation is not just to be a witness of God's deeds to the nation, but to bring them salvation through his own career. He does not witness by being saved, but saves by being humiliated and eliminated. If the servant of these passages is Israel, then it is not the same Israel to whom the prophet speaks in the rest of his prophecy.

Much about the servant passages suggests Second Isaiah himself is the subject. The description of the servant's vocation in the second and third passages clearly fits a prophet. The first person speeches are woven with echoes of Jeremiah's language about his career. Several of the prophets spoke both to Israel and to the nations. Is 42:1–4 a record of a decision of God in the divine assembly to make Second Isaiah his servant by extending his original call (cf. 40:1–8)? Is 49:1–6 the prophet's report of that revision to those to whom he is now sent? Is 50:4–9 his assertion of his faithfulness in the face of severe opposition to his new commission from his own people, or the Babylonians? Is 52:13—53:12 the divine and human response to his martyrdom (perhaps composed by disciples whose work is reflected in parts of chapters 56—66)? If these questions are answered in the affirmative, then we are confronted with a prophetic career unlike any other in Israel. No other prophet is called "my servant" by God (only prophets as a group are called "servants of the Lord"). The designation and commission given in 42:1–4 are usually associated with governing and royal persons. Unlike Jeremiah this servant sees his humilitation as the will of God. His suffering is vicarious. God is glorified in him. His mission is realized beyond the grave. Can this be the same prophet who was the herald of good tidings to the exiles, who announced their return and restoration and their life of blessing and peace in the midst of the nations? The portrait of the servant does not fit easily with the message of Second Isaiah.

The role of "Servant of the Lord," first applied to the exilic community in Second Isaiah's prophecy, undergoes a profound development in the servant passages. The purpose of God for his people and the vocation given the prophet are brought together in the creation of a new office unlike anything else in the Old Testament. Though it has lines of connection with both, it extends and transcends them in a surprising and unexpected way. Through this servanthood the sin of the world is brought within the sphere of God's judgment and salvation. The power by which this servant works is the spiritual energy released when he accepts the suffering his mission involves as punishment for the sake of all. Outside any cultic sphere or ritual he enacts a sacrifice in his own career. Without office in government or empire he becomes the exalted person to whom rulers and people look for righteousness.

While the servant passages give every appearance of having been written by Second Isaiah (with some uncertainty about the fourth passage), they are clearly a distinct stratum in the collection of his sayings. They were incorporated after the corpus received its first arrangement. The material which follows the first three seems to have been written or redacted by those who inserted them (42:5–9; 49:7–12; 50:10–11 and perhaps also 51:1–8; estimates of this material differ). The servant passages must represent a later stage of Second Isaiah's prophecy when some tragedy in his own career and a deepened understanding of God's purpose formed the circumstances in which they were spoken. But to say that much is to guess; their origin is hidden in mystery.

The question about the historical purpose of the servant passages has given birth to a mutlitude of hypotheses and a small library of literature. The question is no modern preoccupation. It arose as early as the redaction of the corpus. The addition of the name "Israel" to 49:3 was perhaps the first attempt to answer the question, and those who translated the Book of Isaiah into Greek agreed by adding the names Jacob/Israel to 42:1 in their version. On the other hand, one of the attachments to the servant passages (50:10–11), seems to portray the servant as an individual. Two other expansions, 48:16 and 51:16a, apparently hold the same opinion. The question puzzled interpreters in New Testament times. The Ethiopian eunuch of Acts 8 was reading Isaiah 53 and asked Philip, "About whom, pray, does the prophet say this, about himself, or about someone else?"

So the final form of the prophecy does not answer the question. Instead, it preserves and proclaims two forms of the Servant of the Lord. One is the role of the people of God who in their human helplessness in the midst of history hear the good tidings of salvation and are summoned to witness to the nations that the Lord alone is God and Savior. They know that the word of the Lord will not return to him empty, but accomplish his purpose. Even in the worst of times they go out in joy and are led forth in peace. The other is the role of one whose ear is opened by God to learn the word that sustains the weary and with it brings light to the nations. In obedience to his work he does not hide his face from shame and spitting. He suffers, is executed, buried, but in his travail he bears the sin of all. His weakness in the world turns out to be victory for the sake of the world. The two forms cannot be separated or merged. The second comes from the first, and the first finds its way in the second.

Whose is the second role? There is only one way to know. Someone must be found, who when we see him, compels and allows us to say "All we like sheep have gone astray; we have turned everyone to his own way; and the Lord has laid on him the iniquity of us all" (53:6).

A good treatment of the exilic period is available in John Bright, *A History of Israel,* second edition (Philadelphia: Westminster, 1972). A somewhat different reconstruction of the period is offered by Siegfried Herrmann, *A History of Israel in Old Testament Times* (Philadelphia: Fortress, 1975) and Martin Noth, *The History of Israel,* second edition (New York: Harper and Row, 1960). For a thorough, cautious reconstruction of Israel's history and religion in the sixth century, see Peter R. Ackroyd, *Exile and Restoration* (Philadelphia: Westminster, 1968).

Two recent commentaries on Ezekiel provide the exegete with rich resources. Walther Eichrodt, *Ezekiel: A Commentary,* The Old Testament Library (Philadelphia: Westminster, 1970) reflects the author's masterful grasp of Old Testament theology and contains stimulating reflections on the theological issues present in the texts. An English translation of Walther Zimmerli, *Ezechiel,* Biblischer Kommentar Altes Testament, volume 13 (Neukirchener Verlag, 1969) is being published by Fortress Press in the *Hermeneia* series. This exhaustive commentary will surely hold its position as the indispensable resource for serious study of Ezekiel for the foreseeable future. The user must be prepared for demanding work. A summary of Zimmerli's interpretation of Ezekiel is available in "The Message of the Prophet Ezekiel," *Interpretation* 23 (1969) 131–157. Andrew B. Davidson, *The Book of The Prophet Ezekiel,* revised edition, Cambridge Bible (Cambridge University, 1916) offers solid guidance in determining the sense of the text.

Among the recent commentaries on Isaiah 40–55, Claus Westermann, *Isaiah 40–66* (Philadelphia: Westminster, 1969) is the best on form-critical and theological matters. Christopher R. North,

The Second Isaiah (Oxford: Clarendon, 1964) is useful in dealing with the language and problems of the Hebrew Text. James Muilenburg, "The Book of Isaiah, Chapters 40–66," *The Interpreter's Bible,* volume 5 (Nashville: Abingdon, 1956) is especially valuable for its analysis of the aesthetic and rhetorical features of the poetry. John L. McKenzie, *Second Isaiah,* Anchor Bible 20 (New York: Doubleday, 1974) is a sound general guide to these chapters. The older works of George Adam Smith, *The Book of Isaiah,* Expositor's Bible, 2 volumes, revised edition (New York: Harper, 1927), and John Skinner, *The Book of the Prophet Isaiah*, Cambridge Bible (Cambridge University, 1915) offer help for exposition.

For treatment of Ezekiel and Second Isaiah in the context of Old Testament theology read Gerhard von Rad, *Old Testament Theology,* volume 2 (New York: Harper and Row, 1965), pages 220–277.

94